THE UK
TEDDY BEA
GUIDE 20(

THE UK
TEDDY BEAR
GUIDE 2008

Further copies
are available from the publisher
Hugglets, PO Box 290, Brighton, England, BN2 1DR
Single copies: UK £7.50, Europe £8.50, Rest of World £10.50 inc postage

ISBN-13: 978-1-870880-35-0
ISSN 0952-8105

Cover Photo: Courtesy Bell Bears (see page 117)

Published by: Hugglets, PO Box 290, Brighton, England, BN2 1DR
Tel: 01273 697974   Fax: 01273 626255   Email: info@hugglets.co.uk

Printed in Great Britain by Newman Thomson, Burgess Hill, England

The UK Teddy Bear Guide 2008 is compiled and published by
Glenn & Irene Jackman, Hugglets, October 2007.

Great care has been taken to ensure the accuracy of information given and it is believed to be correct at the time of going to press. However, no liability can be accepted for loss or damage resulting from error or omission of any sort. Information is invited to ensure the future accuracy and comprehensive coverage of the Guide.

Readers are required to satisfy themselves on all matters concerning advertisers' standards, products and services, and no liability will be accepted by Hugglets in any way.

Welcome to the Guide

Welcome to the twenty-first issue of Hugglets' UK Teddy Bear Guide

● Hugglets comes of age with this twenty first edition which prompts us to look back at our beginnings. Hugglets started when we launched our traditional mohair bears in 1985. Soon we identified the need for a publication to meet the demand for accurate information to serve the developing teddy bear hobby. Our first Guide came out in October 1987. Since then we've up-dated it each year with hundreds of address changes, new businesses, fresh websites, emails and product information.

● Hugglets Festivals have also passed a milestone. When we counted up the number of events held since since Teddies '89 we found we've just passed our 50th! Hugglets currently organises two Festivals each year at London's Kensington Town Hall (February 24th and September 14th in 2008) where you can see many of the shops, artists and bears which appear in this Guide. Complimentary tickets and tips for visitors are included at the back.

● Talking of milestones, the Guide is officially published on October 27th which is the birthday of Teddy Roosevelt whose 150th takes place in 2008. Teddy Roosevelt's association with bears came about through a set of political cartoons beginning in 1902 which led to the newly invented toy becoming known as the Teddy Bear.

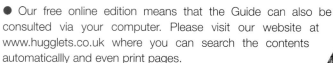

● Changes to the Guide this year include the merging of international entries with UK listings, all marked with a globe image. Makers of gollies, animals and other creations are now included with Bear Makers and Artists. The Bear Gallery has again expanded - now with 112 entries showing the wonderful creativity of bear artists and the variety of their designs.

● Our free online edition means that the Guide can also be consulted via your computer. Please visit our website at www.hugglets.co.uk where you can search the contents automaticallly and even print pages.

Out very best wishes for your bear collecting in 2008.

Glenn & Irene Jackman
Hugglets Publishing

PS. Please remember to mention the Guide whenever you contact advertisers.

Many of the shops listed here are specialist teddy bear shops, but we also include toy and gift shops which have a range of bears on sale.

Readers are advised to telephone for stock details and opening times before travelling a distance. The Teddy Bear Trail section also gives location and stock information.

Some entries are 'mail order only' or dealers to visit by appointment. Some international entries are also included and are indicated by a globe.

• Collectors of old bears should turn to page 42.
• Many bear artists also sell directly - see page 105.

● ABBEY BEARS
11 The Market, Padstow, Cornwall, PL28 8AL
☎ 01841 532484
email: abbeybears@hotmail.co.uk
Please see display advertisement.

● ABBEY BEARS
Fore Street, East Looe, Cornwall, PL13 1DT
☎ 01503 265441
Please see display advertisement.

● ABRACADABRA TEDDY BEARS
8A Cross Street, Saffron Walden, Essex, CB10 1EX
☎ 01799 527222 Fax: As tel.
email: marsha@abracadabra-teddies.com
web: www.abracadabra-teddies.com
Artist bears our speciality, shop exclusives, top brands, vintage, orphanage, dolls, realistic animals, flexible layaway, mail order worldwide, loyalty discounts.

ALLSORTS OF BEARS

Shop 4 Marine View, The Promenade, Cromer, Norfolk, NR27 9HE
☎ 01263 514111
email: info@allsortsofbears.com
web: www.allsortsofbears.com
Steiff, Dean's, Merrythought, Robin Rive, Hermann Spielwaren, Boyds, Cotswold, many shop exclusive artist bears. Interest free layaway. Bears sent worldwide.

APPLE PIE HOUSE LTD

8 New Street, Ledbury, Herefordshire, HR8 2DX
☎ 01531 635290 Fax: 020 8662 0601
email: shop@applepiehouse.com
web: www.applepiehouse.com
Teddy Bear Heaven since 1997.

ARCTOPHILIA

120 West Street, Faversham, Kent, ME13 7JB
☎ 01795 597770 Fax: As tel.
web: www.arctophilia.com
Teddy bears and beanies galore. Prices for all pockets. Mail order available. Open Tuesday to Saturday. See display advertisement.

ARUNDEL TEDDY BEARS

☎ 0776 997 7195
email: info@arundelteddybears.co.uk
web: www.arundelteddybears.co.uk
A leading specialist teddy bear shop since 1991. Steiff, Dean's, Hermann limited editions, and much more.

ASHBY BEARS
& COLLECTABLES

Rushtons Yard, Off Market Street, Ashby-de-la Zouch, Leicestershire, LE65 1AL
☎ 01530 564444
email: sales@ashbybears.com
web: www.ashbybears.com
East Midlands largest selection. Club store for most leading manufacturers. Purchase securely on our hugely popular web site www.ashbybears.com

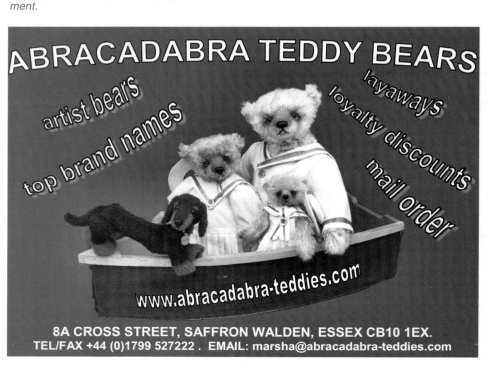

ABRACADABRA TEDDY BEARS

artist bears
top brand names
layaways
loyalty discounts
mail order

www.abracadabra-teddies.com

8A CROSS STREET, SAFFRON WALDEN, ESSEX CB10 1EX.
TEL/FAX +44 (0)1799 527222 . EMAIL: marsha@abracadabra-teddies.com

Hugglets PUBLISHING

● ASHWOOD NURSERIES GIFT SHOP

Ashwood Lower Lane, Kingswinford, West Midlands, DY6 0AE
☎ 01384 401996 Fax: 01384 401108
email: info@ashwoodnurseries.com
web: www.ashwoodnurseries.com
Steiff Club Store, also Robin Rive, Zena Arts and soft toys available. Open every day. Tea rooms. Worldwide mail-order service.

● ASQUITHS World Famous Teddy Bear Shops

ETON 33 High Street Eton
Berkshire SL4 6AX Tel: 01753 831200
HENLEY 2-4 New Street
Henley-on-Thames
Oxen RG9 2BT Tel: 01491 571978
sales@asquiths.com
www.asquiths.com
ASQUITHS 'World Famous' Teddy Bear Shops are located in the quintessentially English towns of Henley-on-Thames, and Eton by Windsor. The shops are open 7 days a week and are full of the World's finest bears from leading artists and top manufacturers. We are Club Stores for both Steiff and Hermann, and have our own Arctophiles Club for collectors to get the best in bears. Also in store for you are fabrics, prints, passports, stationery, and a comprehensive selection of teddy bear clothing. We repair and restore teddies back to health, and when Joan is not running the shops or talking about teddies on the local BBC radio, she designs ASQUITHS Luxury Teddy Bears which are in some of the country's most prestigious households. So bear in mind a visit to ASQUITHS and be in good company.

● B-BEARS AND GIFTS

10 Woolworths Market Place, Albany Creek, Brisbane, Queensland 4053, Australia
☎ +61 (0)7 3325 5366 Fax: +61 (0)7 3325 5388
email: info@BearsAndGifts.com.au
web: www.BearsAndGifts.com.au
Ranked No. 1 plush website in the world. Thousands of teddy bears and gifts for every occasion. Fast, easy delivery worldwide. See display advertisement.

● BACTON BEARS

at Jeffries Country Clothing, Station Garage, Bacton, Stowmarket, Suffolk, IP14 4HP
☎ 01449 781087 Fax: 01449 780391
email: bactonbears@aol.com
web: www.bactonbears.co.uk
Literally hundreds of bears!

● BAR STREET BEARS

30 Bar Street, Scarborough, North Yorkshire, YO11 2HT
☎ 01723 353636
Please see display advertisement.

● BÄRENBOUTIQUE

Scheuerner Str. 59, 76593 Gernsbach, Germany
☎ +49 (0)1577 316 26 46
email: info@baerenboutique.de
web: www.baerenboutique.de
Germany's no.1 dealer of Hermann Coburg bears. Plus Teddy Hermann, Deb Canham, Clemens Spieltiere, Martin Sonneberg. Well-priced, fast, reliable.

● THE BEAR EMPORIUM

Well View, Ridgeway Craft Centre, Ridgeway, Nr Sheffield, Derbyshire, S12 3XR
☎ 01142 482010   web: www.bear-emporium.com
For all your beary needs. Stockists of major leading makers. Bear gifts for all occasions. Teddy hospital.

● THE BEAR GARDEN

10 Jeffries Passage, Guildford, Surrey, GU1 4AP
☎ 01483 302581 Fax: 01483 457393
email: bears@beargarden.co.uk
web: www.beargarden.co.uk
Established 1992. Leading UK teddy bear specialist. Experts in Steiff, Deans and other quality teddy bear manufacturers and leading bear artists.

● THE BEAR HUGGERY

Tower House, Castle Street, Douglas, Isle of Man, IM1 2EZ ☎ 01624 676333/07624 490551
email: bearhuggery@manx.net
web: www.thebearhuggery.co.uk
Special bears & animals to love! Artist, vintage, teddy hospital, favourite manufacturers, one-offs and exclusives! Come and have a hug!

● BEAR IT IN MIND

High Street, Beaulieu, Hampshire, SO42 7YA
☎ 01590 612097
email: info@bearitinmind.com
web: www.bearitinmind.com
Collectable bears in the New Forest including all major names, artist corner, exclusive jewellery line, candles and other related gifts.

● THE BEAR PATCH

33 Market Place, Ashbourne, Derbyshire, DE6 1EU
☎ 01335 342391
email: pauline@thebearpatch.co.uk
web: www.thebearpatch.co.uk
Huge selection including Steiff, Dean's, Merrythought, Charlie Bears, Robin Rive, Steiner, Deb Canham, Hermann, Gund, Kosen, artist bears, old bears.

● BEAR PATHS

2815 Jay Avenue, Cleveland, OH 44113, USA
☎ +1 216 566 1519 Fax: +1 216 566 7924
email: bearpaths@aol.com web: www.bearpaths.com
More than 500 artist bears online. Join Plum Club today - it's free - and an Internet show every Monday!

THE BEAR SHOP

3 Sir Isaacs Walk, Colchester, Essex, CO1 1JJ
☎ 01206 577345
email: enquiries@bearshops.co.uk
web: www.bearshops.co.uk
Cuddles and collectables, artist bears and limited editions. New bears always arriving. Visit or telephone for information. Open Mon-Sat 10am-5pm. See display advertisement.

THE BEAR SHOP

18 Elm Hill, Norwich, Norfolk, NR3 1HN
☎ 01603 766866 Fax: 01603 618619
email: enquiries@bearshops.co.uk
web: www.bearshops.co.uk
Exclusive teddy bear shop in Norwich. All famous makes plus many artist bears. Please send for free catalogue or see website. Open 7 days.

BEARS 'N' THINGS

8 Royal Arcade, Wigan, Lancashire, WN1 1QH
☎ 01942 234222   email: info@bearsnthings.co.uk
web: www.bearsnthings.co.uk
Steiff, Hermann, Gund, most major manufacturers and artists, gollies and gifts galore.

BEARS & STITCHES

4 Cumberland Street, Woodbridge, Suffolk, IP12 4AB
☎ 01394 388999 Fax: As tel.
Steiff, Robin Rive, Gund, Russ and others. Also doll's house furniture and crafts.

THE BEARS DEN

Craft Corner, 6 Riverside Precinct, Corporation Street, Rotherham, South Yorkshire, S60 1ND
☎ **01709 828619**
email: **thebearsden@topliss123.fsnet.co.uk**
Yorkshire's friendliest bear shop. Steiff and leading manufacturers and now stocking Charlie Bears. Artist bears, layaway service, gifts and crafts.

BEARS ON THE SQUARE

2 The Square, Ironbridge, Shropshire, TF8 7AQ
☎ 01952 433924 Fax: 01952 433926
email: bernie@bearsonthesquare.com
web: www.bearsonthesquare.com
The Midland's largest selection of bears from major manufacturers and leading artists. Many shop exclusives. Worldwide mail order service.

BEARS TO COLLECT

Tilbrook Mill, B645, Lower Dean, Nr Kimbolton, Huntingdon, Cambridgeshire, PE28 0LH
☎ 01480 860376 Fax: 01480 861025
email: shirley@bears2collect.co.uk
web: www.bears2collect.co.uk
Specialists in limited edition and collectable bears. Exclusive range of artist bears, t-shirts, china and limited edition teddy bear prints.

C J BEAVIS LTD

14-16 The Arcade, Bedford, Bedfordshire, MK40 1NS
☎ 01234 353741 Fax: 01234 330028
email: michael@cjbeavis.co.uk
web: www.beavis-shops.co.uk
Steiff and Gund stockist.

I C BEAVIS LTD

Upper Saint James Street, Newport, Isle of Wight, PO30 1LG
☎ 01983 523271 Fax: 01983 532168
email: michael@icbeavis.co.uk
web: www.beavis-shops.co.uk
Steiff and Gund stockist.

BROUGHTY BEARS

The Growling Part of McDonald the Stationer, 228-230 Brook Street, Broughty Ferry, Dundee, Tayside, DD5 2AH
☎ 01382 477567 Fax: As tel.
email: fenella@broughtybears.co.uk
web: www.broughtybears.co.uk
Steiff Club Store, stocking Robin Rive, Gund, Dean's, Hermann/Spielwaren, Merrythought, Pooh figures by Enesco and much much more.

BUCKS BEARS

The Barn, Westhorpe Farm, Little Marlow, Buckinghamshire, SL7 3RQ
☎ 01628 472735
email: info@bucks-bears.co.uk
web: www.bucks-bears.co.uk
A little secret shop with a big surprise inside. Experience our wonderful shop with hassle free parking in peaceful surroundings.

THE CALICO TEDDY

USA ☎ +1 410 433 9202 Fax: +1 410 433 9203
email: calicteddy@aol.com
web: www.calicoteddy.com
Please see display advertisement

Hugglets PUBLISHING

Bear Paths

2815 Jay Avenue
Cleveland, Ohio 44113, USA

Shop at www.bearpaths.com

Visit our on-line gallery filled with more than 500 Artist Bears.
Be sure to visit the new Orphans section of our website.
Register for our exclusive Plum Club. It's the only way
to experience a virtual Artist Bear Show every week.

World Wide
Shipping Available

Tel 1-216-566-1519
Fax 1-216-566-7924
E-mail: bearpaths@aol.com

CAROL'S TINY TREASURES

13 High Street, Chipping Sodbury, Bristol, Avon, BS37 6BA

☎ 01454 318573

email: info@carolstinytreasures.co.uk

web: www.carolstinytreasures.co.uk

Stocking: Steiff, Gund, Dean's, Charlie Bears, Hermann, Robin Rive, Rainbow Designs. Dollshouses/ furniture/ lighting/ accessories. See our Miniature Fun Fair.

CAUSEWAY HOUSE CRAFTS AND CINNAMON BEAR COFFEE SHOP

Castleton, Hope Valley, Derbyshire, S33 8WE

☎ 01433 620343 Fax: 01433 620258

email: enquiries@cinnamon-bear.co.uk

web: www.cinnamon-bear.co.uk

Join us in our coffee shop and find a new friend amongst Steiff, Robin Rive and Deb Canham bears.

CE GIFTS & BEARS

5 Hebden Court, Matlock St, Bakewell, Derbyshire, DE45 1EE

☎ 01629 814811 Fax: 01629 814820

email: info@cegifts.co.uk

web: www.cegifts.co.uk

Large selection of collector and plush bears. Also beautiful giftware and dolls house accessories. Secure internet shopping and layaway available.

CEJAIS BEARS & DOLLSHOUSES

169 Medieval Spon Street, Coventry, Warwickshire, CV1 3BB

☎ 024 76 633630

email: collect@cejais.co.uk

web: www.cejais.net

Dean's, Steiff, Gund, Cotswold, Russ, Robin Rive, Merrythought, Charlie Bears, Heartfelt, Boyds, Teddy Bear Orphanage.

TEDDY BEAR SHOP

A LITTLE SECRET SHOP WITH A BIG SURPRISE INSIDE

at WESTHORPE FARM, LITTLE MARLOW, BUCKS, SL7 3RQ

and many many more

www.bucks-bears.co.uk

Telephone: 01628 472735

CHILDHOOD FANTASIES

314 West King Street, Martinsburg, 25401, USA
☎ +1 304 260 0658 Fax: +1 304 260 0558
email: martichildhood@aol.com
web: www.childhoodfantasiesbear.com
Steiff, Hermann, Merrythought, Dean's, Deb Canham, Clemens, Cooperstown. Your shoppe for quality bears and service since 1987. We ship internationally.

● CHRISTMAS ANGELS

47 Low Petergate, York, North Yorkshire, YO1 7HT
☎ 01904 639908 Fax: 01904 613640
email: sales@christmasangels.co.uk
web: www.christmasangels.co.uk
Wide selection of artist bears and limited edition bears in stock in our upstairs gallery. Open every day.

● COBBLESTONE BEARS AND GIFTS

Blakemere Craft Centre, Chester Road, Sandiway, Cheshire, CW8 2EB
☎ 01606 889192 Fax: 01606 301495
email: ginny@blakemere-shoppingexperience.com
web: www.blakemere-shoppingexperience.com
Collectables and bear related gifts.

● CUDDLY KERRLECTABLES

78 High Street, Invergordon, Ross-shire, IV18 0DL
☎ 01349 854256 Fax: 01349 854114
email: beaulyinsurance@aol.com
Unique Bruijntje Bears, Steiff, huge range Charlie Bears, Isabelle Collection, Merrythought, Hermann, Deb Canham etc. Our prices can't be beaten!

● CURTIS BRAE OF STRATFORD

32 Sheep Street, Stratford upon Avon, Warwickshire, CV37 6EE
☎ 01789 267277
email: sales@curtisbrae.co.uk
web: www.curtisbrae.co.uk
Specialist shop for teddy bears and Russian nesting dolls. Packed with bears from all our favourite manufacturers and local artists.

DAISA ORIGINAL DESIGNS LTD

Appletree Lodge, Westfield Lakes, Barton-upon-Humber, North Lincolnshire, DN18 5RG
☎ 01652 661881 Fax: 01652 661882
email: sales@itsadodl.com
web: www.theoriginalreikibear.com and www.itsadodl.com
Please see 'It's a dodl' © display advertisement.

DOLLY DAYDREAMS

Elm Park Garden Centre, Aldermaston Road, Pamber End, Hampshire, RG26 5QN
☎ 01256 889111
email: enquiries@dollydaydreams.net
web: www.dollydaydreams.net
Largest stock of Dolls, Bears and Dolls' House Miniatures in the South of England! Shop open every day including Sundays.

DOLLY DOMAIN OF SOUTH SHIELDS

45 Henderson Road, Simonside, South Shields, Tyne & Wear, NE34 9QW
☎ 0191 42 40 400 Lo-call: 0845 6655 667
Fax: 0191 42 40 400
email: shop@dollydomain.com
web: www.dollydomain.com
Please see display advertisement. 'User friendly' website, world wide mail orders, lo-call phone number, best priced stocks in Northeast England.

DOLLY LAND

864 Green Lanes, Winchmore Hill, London, N21 2RS
☎ 020 8360 1053 mob: 07940 205 928
Fax: 020 8364 1370
email: greta_dollyland@yahoo.co.uk
web: www.dolly-land.co.uk
We stock bears: old limited edition Steiff you are missing, Hermann, Merrythought, gollies, antique dolls, Annette Himstedt, trains, diecast, scalectric.

DREAM HOUSE

4 rue Beaumont, 06300 Nice, France
☎ +33 (0)4 93 55 09 16
email: dreamhousenice@yahoo.fr
web: www.nicenounours.com
Probably the largest selection of teddy bear products on the Cote d'Azur. Un choix enorme plus Me to You.

● GERALDINE'S OF EDINBURGH

☎ 0131 333 1833
email: geraldine.e@virgin.net
web: www.dollsandteddies.com
Specialists in mohair bears from childrens' heirlooms to collectors' limited editions. Mail orders always welcome.

● THE GIFT

5 Kirkgate, Newark, Nottinghamshire, NG24 1AD
☎ 01636 610075
email: info@thegift-newarkbears.com
web: www.thegiftbears.com
Over 200 different bears in stock including Steiff, Dean's, Robin Rive, miniatures and gollies. Many discontinued available at discounted prices!

● GOLDILOCKS

4 The Mall, Ringwood Road, Burley, Ringwood, Hampshire, BH24 4BS
☎ 01425 403558 Fax: As tel.
email: carolinewaud@goldilocksbears.co.uk
web: www.teddybearsofburley.co.uk
Good selection of bears at all prices including Steiff, Dean's, Hermann, Merrythought, Robin Rive, Cotswold, Isabelle Collection and Charlie Bears.

● GORGE BEAR COMPANY

Cheddar Gorge, Somerset, BS27 3QE
☎ 01934 743333
email: headbear@bear-world.com
web: www.bear-world.com
Please see advert page 25.

● GRANNY'S GOODIES

Unit 3, 34a Camden Passage/Islington Green, London, N1 8DU

☎ 020 8693 5432 or 020 7704 2210 (shop)
Fax: 020 8693 5432
email: klaregerwat-clark@tinyworld.co.uk
web: www.grannysgoodiesfairs.com
Antique & artist bears. Brenda Gerwat-Clark. Open Wednesday and Saturday only. 8.30 - 4.00. Also teddy bear hospital.

● GRETA MAY ANTIQUES

The New Curiosity Shop, 7 Tollgate Buildings, Hadlow Road, Tonbridge, Kent, TN9 1NX
☎ 01732 366730 mob 0783 6633 521
email: gretamayantiques@hotmail.com
A treasure trove of antiques and collectables, brought alive with the personality, charm, of artist, antique and character bears.

● HALCYON OF ST. MARYCHURCH

42B Fore Street, St. Marychurch, Torquay, Devon, TQ1 4LX
☎ 01803 314958
email: dinahowell@btconnect.com
web: www.halcyonbears.com
An exciting range of bears.

● HAMLEYS OF LONDON

188-196 Regent Street, London, W1R 6BT
☎ 020 7479 7308 Fax: 020 7479 7398
web: www.hamleys.com
Hamley's exclusive limited edition bears. Comprehensive range of collector bears. Specialist Steiff consultant. World-wide mail order service available.

● HARTLEY'S OF LEYBURN

3 High Street, Leyburn, North Yorkshire, DL8 5AH
☎ 01969 622209
email: info@hartleybears.co.uk
web: www.hartleybears.co.uk
Formally Hartley Bear's Emporium retailer of hand made and manufactured bears and gifts.

● HEAVENLY CREATIONS

43 Christchurch Road, Ringwood, Hampshire, BH24 1DG
☎ 01425 470654 / 470422
email: kingstonbears@aol.com
web: www.kingstonbears.com
By appointment only. The home of Kingston Bears.

● THE HEN NEST

207 North Main Street, Columbia, AL 36319, USA
☎ +1 334 696 3480/334 696 4390 Fax: +1 800 452 1273 ORDERS
email: hennest@aol.com
web: www.hennest.com
Current and retired selections from R John Wright, Steiff, Deb Canham, Karl Gibbons Collection, Little Gems, Hermann, and Artist Bears.

● HOLDINGHAM BEARS

Unit 6, Navigation Yard, Carre Street, Sleaford, Lincolnshire, NG34 7TR
☎ 01529 303266
email: barbara@holdinghambears.com
web: www.holdinghambears.com
Watch Barbara Daughtrey designing and making quality collectors bears in her new workshop situated in the HUB courtyard. Commissions accepted.

● INSPIRATIONS

21 High Street, Aldershot, Hampshire, GU11 1BH
☎ 01252 336677
email: enquiries@inspirationsgiftshop.co.uk
web: www.inspirationsgiftshop.co.uk
Located on the Hampshire/Surrey border, we stock a variety of bears including Steiff, Gund, Boyds, Cotswold and Ty.

● JU-BEARY BEARS

Studio 3, Barleylands Craft Village, Barleylands Road, Billericay, Essex, CM11 2UD
☎ 01268 525775
email: jubearybears@hotmail.co.uk
Come and visit the Ju-Beary Bears Studio. Open 11am til 4pm Wednesday to Sunday. Layaway service. Also Pooh, Cherished Teddies.

World of Bears
& The Gorgeous Bear Co

and Friends

Elaine at The Gorge Bear Co and World of Bears would like to extend an invitation for you to visit her and her many beary friends, over eighteen thousand in fact! Don't be surprised if your breath is taken away as you enter either of her shops. The Gorge Bear Co and World of Bears renowned for being the best and biggest teddy bear shop most people will have ever visited.

DEAN'S
Britain's Oldest Teddy Bear Maker

Steiff
BUTTON IN EAR

CHARLIE BEARS

ty

Teddy

Hermann

Gotta Gotta GUND

RUSS
make someone happy

HANSA
Toy Leader Kingdom

MERRYTHOUGHT

Isabelle Collection

Robin Rive

JELLYCAT

SESAME STREET

Garfield

There is something suitable for everyone, from young to old, and something for everyones budget. Both stores have areas dedicated to each major manufacturer, with most of the ranges on display. this combined with excellant knowledge makes her stores the leading specialist "teddy bear and friends" retailer in the UK.

World of Bears
Top Left: Part of the impressive 2nd floor showroom
Right: Part of Animal Kingdom
Middle Left: Part of the Boyds Attic
Bottom Left: Cheddar Store

Ba pu s

ANIMAL KINGDOM
NOW OPEN !

World of Bears,
20 Lower Middle Street,
Taunton, Somerset, UK
(01823) 332050

Over 18,000 bruins, animals and soft toys in stock! If you cannot visit us in person then visit our fantastic website

The Gorge Bear Co,
Cheddar, Somerset, UK
(01934) 743333

www.worldofbears.com

HALCYON
COLLECTIONS

TEDDIES
TO
TREASURE

- Dean's ● Merrythought,
  - Cotswold ● Russ
- Local specialist makers
- Some discontinued bears
- Dolls Houses ● Pottery

42b Fore Street, St Marychurch,
Devon, TQ1 4LX Tel: 01803 314958

See our updated website
www.halcyonbears.com
Give Diana a ring

Visit www.kingswearbears.com

for free UK
delivery

Or in the fur at:
**Kingswear Bears
2a The Square
Kingswear
Dartmouth
Devon
TQ6 0AA
01803 752632**

See our main entry for more details

● KIERON JAMES DESIGNS
79 High Street, Lindfield, West Sussex, RH16 2HN
☎ 01444 484870 Fax: 01444 484890
email: kieron.james@talk21.com
A shop in picturesque Lindfield village for fine teddy bears and gifts. Steiff, Hermann, etc. Credit, debit cards accepted.

● KINGSWEAR BEARS AND FRIENDS
2A The Square, Kingswear, Dartmouth, Devon, TQ6 0AA
☎ **01803 752632**
email: teddies@kingswearbears.com
web: www.kingswearbears.com
Free UK delivery. Riverside shop opposite steam railway. New Boyds ranges, Charlie Bears, Steiff, Dean's, Hermann, Robin Rive & more.

● KOKO'S BEAR SHOP
44 Union Street, Ryde, Isle of Wight, PO33 2LF
☎ 01983 616815
email: sales@kokosbearshop.com
web: www.kokosbearshop.com
Extensive range from affordable cuddlies to unique handmade artist collections and limited edition miniatures! Buy online. Flexible layaway service available.

● L'OURS DU MARAIS
18 Rue Pavée, 75004 Paris, France
☎ +33 (0)1 42 77 60 43 Fax: +33 (0)1 42 77 60 44
email: oursdumarais@wanadoo.fr
web: www.oursdumarais.com
The first teddy bear shop in Paris. Many bears by French and international artists. Steiff and Hermann club shop.

● LATIMER OF BEWDLEY
2 Sandstone Road, Bewdley, Worcestershire, DY12 1BW
☎ 01299 404000 Fax: As tel.
email: latimerofbewdley@aol.com
web: www.latimerofbewdley.com
Teddy bear manufacturers and importers. Suitable for the Gift and Souvenir trade.

HAMLEYS, the world's finest toy brand was established in London in 1760, and today is home to bears of all shapes, sizes, colours, with something to suit all ages and occasions.

Our Collectable Range includes bears from Steiff, Hermann and Merrythought alongside Artist Bears from My Old Ted, Hardy, Hoo Bears, Bedspring Bears and lots more.

We also carry shop exclusives and one offs and offer a Worldwide mail order service.

For more information please contact **Libby Baldry**.
Tel: 020 7479 7308 Fax: 020 7479 7398
www.hamleys.com

● LEIGH TOY FAIR

45 Broadway West, Leigh-on-Sea, Essex, SS9 2BX
☎ 01702 473288 Fax: As tel.
email: info@leightoyfair.co.uk
web: www.leightoyfair.co.uk
Steiff Club 'best of' store, Dean's, Merrythought, Hermann, Deb Canham, Silver Cross prams, dolls houses, castles, forts, traditional wooden toys.

● LET'S GO ROUND AGAIN

2 Maypole Street, Wombourne, West Midlands, WV5 9J ☎ 01902 324141
email: letsgoroundagain@hotmail.co.uk
Bears by Steiff, Dean's, Hermann, Robin Rive Gollies & much more at our lovely village shop. Mail order and layaway scheme.

● LIFE LIKE FRIENDS

12-13 Harris Arcade, Reading, Berkshire, RG1 1DN
☎ 0118 956 8877 Fax: 0118 956 8899
email: enquiries@lifelikefriends.co.uk
web: www.lifelikefriends.co.uk
Realistic cuddly toy animals, puppets, miniature collectable animals and teaching aids. Order online or visit our shop in Reading.

● LITTLE PAWS

4 Castle Street, Ludlow, Shropshire, SY8 1AT
☎ 01584 875286
email: teddy@littlepawsludlow.co.uk
web: www.littlepawsludlow.co.uk
An excellent selection of traditional one-offs and limited editions, artist bears, gollies, miniatures and shop exclusives including Canterbury, Clemens, Merrythought.

● MARY SHORTLE

9 Lord Mayors Walk, York, North Yorkshire, also at 5 Bootham, York and 9, 15 & 17 Queen's Arcade, Leeds.
☎ 01904 425168 / 631165 / 634045; Tel: 01132 456160 (Leeds) Fax: 01904 425168
email: mary@maryshortleofyork.com
web: www.maryshortleofyork.com
Antique and modern teddies. Limited editions, miniature teddies, leading artists. Teddy bear hospital. Hundreds of teddies to choose from.

● MEMORY LANE

69 Wakefield Road, Sowerby Bridge, West Yorkshire, HX6 2UX
☎ 01422 833223 Fax: 01422 835230
email: lynda@memorylanebears.co.uk
web: www.memorylanebears.co.uk
Bears and friends. Please ring Lynda, we may have what you seek. Sensible offers accepted. Open 12-4 everyday, closed Thursday.

● MILFORD MODELS & HOBBIES

48 High Street, Milford-on-Sea, Hampshire, SO41 0QD
☎ 01590 642112 Fax: 01590 645029
email: mmh1@dsl.pipex.com
web: www.milford-models.co.uk
See display advertisement.

Lifelike cuddly toy animals and hand puppets.
Hundreds of animals in stock.

order online
www.lifelikefriends.co.uk

Or visit our shop
12-13 Harris Arcade,
Reading, RG1 1DN.
(100mtrs from
Reading Station).

Tel: +44 (0) 118 956 8877
Email: enquiries@lifelikefriends.co.uk

THE OLDE TEDDY BEAR SHOPPE
10449 Islington Avenue, Box 797, Kleinburg, Ontario, L0J 1C0, Canada
☎ +1 905 893 3590 Fax: +1 905 893 3605
email: info@theoldeteddybearshoppe.com
web: www.theoldeteddybearshoppe.com
Retail shop specialising in artist teddy bears: Forget-Me-Nots, Ingrid Schmid and more, as well as Steiff, R. John Wright, Merrythought.

ORPHAN BEARS
Westcombe Trading Ltd
☎ 01707 649758
email: trade@orphanbears.com
web: www.orphanbears.com
Unique, articulated designer bears in need of a loving home - each with their own story. Contact us for great deals.

● THE OYSTER BOX

Royal Star Arcade, Maidstone, Kent, ME14 1JL
☎ 01622 685423 Fax: 01622 682511
email: theoysterbox@dsl.pipex.com
web: www.theoysterbox.co.uk
Stockists of Steiff Bears. We stock a range of classic and cosy bears including Limited Editions. We offer free delivery.

● PARADE - THE GIFT SHOP

19 Kings Parade, Cambridge, Cambridgeshire, CB2 1SP
☎ 01223 578728
Exclusive outlet for 'Sarah's Bears of Cambridge' and other souvenir bears. Quality gift shop and Steiff club store.

● PARTY BEARS

The Antique Map Shop, 9/10 Pulteney Bridge, Bath, Avon, BA2 4AY
☎ 01225 446097
email: sue@partybears-bath.co.uk
web: www.partybears-bath.co.uk
Please see display advertisement.

● PAWS IN THE FOREST

27 High Street, Lyndhurst, Hampshire, SO43 7BE
☎ 02380 282697
Collectables and bears by Steiff, Robin Rive, Dean's, Hermann, Cliff Richard, Bear Unlimited, Charlie Bears, Hardy Bears, Russ and Trendle.

● SUE PEARSON

18 Brighton Square, The Lanes, Brighton, East Sussex, BN1 1HD
☎ 01273 774851/329247
email: sales@suepearson.co.uk
web: www.suepearson.co.uk
Please see advertisement page 5.

● PEGGOTTY

2805 Barksdale Drive, Plano, Texas 75025, USA
☎ +1 972 491 0104
email: teddy@peggotty.force9.net
web: www.peggotty.f9.co.uk
Portobello bears in stock in both the UK and USA. Please call or see website for location of your favourite bear.

Milford Models & Hobbies

**48 High Street, Milford-on-Sea, near Lymington,
Hants, SO41 0QD   Tel: 01590 642112 Fax: 01590 645029
E.mail: mmh1@dsl.pipex.com
www.milford-models.co.uk**

Steiff Limited Editions

Steiff, Merrythought, Dean's
& Hermann Club Stores

Robin Rive,
Gund, Schuco, Hantel,
Numerous Artist Bears,
Bear related items.

Railways • Diecast • Kits
Britains • Schuco • Bassett-Lowke

STEIFF CLUB

● THE PIED PIPER

1 Montpellier Avenue, Cheltenham, Gloucestershire, GL50 1SA
☎ 01242 251532
email: piedpiperchelt@aol.com
web: www.bearsanddolls.co.uk
Please see display advertisement.

● POSTAL BEARS

6 Atherton Avenue, Mottram, Cheshire, SK14 6NJ
☎ 01457 766650 Fax: As tel.
email: elaine@postalbears.co.uk
web: www.postalbears.co.uk
Secure site, mail order, layaway.

● THE POTTING SHED

Ransoms Garden Centre, St. Martin, Jersey, JE3 6UD
☎ 01534 854203 Fax: As tel.
email: ransoms@localdial.com
Stockist of all major names. Also, own store limited edition Bear and Robin Rive Golly. Steiff club store.

● QVC

Marco Polo House, 346 Queenstown Road, London, SW8 4NQ
☎ 0800 514131
email: webmasteruk@qvc.com
web: www.qvcuk.com
See ad for more details.

● RAZZLE DAZZLE

119 Regent Street, Kingswood, Bristol, Avon, BS15 8LJ
☎ 01179 614141
web: www.razzledazzlegifts.co.uk
The most enchanting shop in the Southwest, stocking Steiff, Dean's, Hermann, Robin Rive, Gund, Hansa, dollshouses and accessories.

● RECOLLECT DOLLS HOSPITAL

17 Junction Road, Burgess Hill, West Sussex, RH15 0HR
☎ 01444 871052 Fax: As tel.
email: dollshopuk@aol.com
web: www.dollshospital.co.uk
Dolls hospital & supplies. Jointed porcelain bears. Bear making supplies.

The place to shop for
exclusive and limited edition teddy bears
from around the world

QVC, the UK's favourite TV shopping channel,
is one of the leading retailers of teddy bears.
Not only do we have a huge choice of
exclusive teddies from all over the world but
also access to a wealth of educated and
trustworthy information about the bears.

The wide range of collectible teddies include
limited editions and exclusives from Steiff,
Hermann Spielwaren and Charlie Bears.

**For further information please call:
QVC Customer Services: 0800 51 41 31
or visit www.qvcuk.com**

THE ROCKING HORSE GALLERY

803 Caroline Street, Fredericksburg, VA 22401, USA
☎ +1 540 371 1894 Fax: +1 540 372 4136
*The world's first Teddy Bear Artist Gallery.
Celebrating it's 25th anniversary.*

● ROUND ABOUT BEARS

The Old Forge, London Road, Nr Brampton, Beccles,
Suffolk, NR34 8EL
☎ 01502 578338 or 07785 788307
email: mille@roundaboutbears.co.uk
web: www.roundaboutbears.co.uk
*Steiff club store specialising in new and old
limited editions from all over the world.
Exclusive stockist of Hovvig. Jill Baxter.*

SARAH BEARS

PO Box 4075, Brekenridge, CO 80424, USA
☎ +1 719 839 5770
email: info@sarahbears.com
web: www.sarahbears.com
*Online artist bear store - purchase directly
online now!*

● SERENDIPITY

53 The Arcade, Piece Hall, Halifax, West Yorkshire,
HX1 1RE
☎ 01422 340097
email: serendipityhalifax@hotmail.com
web: www.tedshop.com
*Stockist of Steiff, Dean's, Hermann,
Merrythought, Ty, Russ, Boyds and others.
Also dolls and accessories, houses and
twelfth scale miniatures.*

● SIXPENNY BEARS

The Square, Hawkshead, Cumbria, LA22 0NZ
☎ 01539 436003
email: janine@sixpennybears.com
web: www.sixpennybears.com
*Visit the specialist bear shop in the Lake
District. All leading manufacturers and
artists. Friendly welcome. Also bear memorabilia.*

● ST MARTIN'S GALLERY

The Old Church, Mockbeggar Lane, Ibsley,
Hampshire, BH24 3PP
☎ 01425 489090
email: stmartins@ibsleyhants.freeserve.co.uk
web: www.stmartinsartandcraftcentre.com
*Set in a 17th century church our bears and
gollies are very well behaved. They include
Robin Rive, Tailored Teddies, Steiner and
many more.*

● STEIFF GALLERY

The Glades, Bromley, Kent, BR1 1DN
☎ 0208 466 8444
email: london@steiff-gallery.co.uk
web: www.steiff-gallery.co.uk
Everything Steiff under one roof.

● THE TEDDY BEAR CLUB STORE

'Exclusives', Great Baddow, Chelmsford, Essex
☎ 08700 347578 Fax: As tel.
email: teddybear@teddybearclub.co.uk
web: www.teddybearclub.co.uk
*Established teddy bear and golly gift
store. Shop securely online for Robin
Rive, Merrythought, Steiner, Gund,
Cotswold and Charlie Bears.*

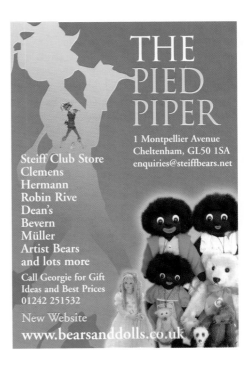

TEDDY BEAR HOLLOW

PO Box 8632, Loughborough, LE11 9DS
☎ 0845 388 3021
email: sales@teddybearhollow.co.uk
web: www.teddybearhollow.com
Online and mail order retailers of limited edition and collectable teddy bears, animals. Children and baby safe items.

TEDDY BEAR HOUSE

The Dorset Teddy Bear Museum, Corner of High East St & Salisbury St, Dorchester, Dorset, DT1 1JU
☎ 01305 263200 Fax: 01305 268885
email: info@teddybearhouse.co.uk
web: www.teddybearhouse.co.uk
Large selection of collectors' bears, limited editions and most leading makes. Steiff, Merrythought and Gund. Something for all tastes.

THE TEDDY BEAR ORPHANAGE

92 Heath Street, Nutgrove, St Helens, Merseyside, WA9 5NJ
☎ 01744 812274 Fax: 01744 813334
email: info@teddybearorphanage.co.uk
web: www.teddybearorphanage.co.uk
Artist, antique and discounted bears.

TEDDY BEARS & FRIENDS OF BOURNE

5a South Street, Bourne, Lincolnshire, PE10 9LY
☎ 01778 426898
email: bournebears@yahoo.co.uk
web: www.bourne-bears.co.uk
Steiff, Merrythought, Deans, Hermann, Cotswold, Charlie Bears, Isabelle Collection, Steiner, Clemens, Robin Rive, Russ, Gund, TY, Gollies, Teddy Bear Hospital.

TEDDY BEARS DOWNSTAIRS

164 Swan Street, Morpeth, Hunter Valley, NSW 2321, Australia
☎ +61 (0)2 4933 9794 Fax: +61 (0)2 4934 3778
email: aussiebear@kooee.com.au
Leading teddy bear and golly shop. With bear related items. The largest shop in Australia situated in historic village of Morpeth.

TEDDY BEARS OF WITNEY

99 High Street, Witney, Oxfordshire, OX28 6HY
☎ **01993 706616 Fax: 01993 702344**
email: **alfonzo@witneybears.co.uk**
web: **www.teddybears.co.uk**
Open 7 days a week. 2008 catalogue (£5) features the new Steiff Centenary Alfonzo and 275 other exclusive limited editions.

TEDDY BEARS' PICKNICK

PO Box 333, 3960 BH Wijk bij Duurstede, Netherlands
☎ +31 (0)343 577068 Fax: As tel.
email: picknick@xs4all.nl
web: www.teddybearspicknick.com
Visit our website to see Steiff, Kosen and Artist Bears and Cats, a.o. Forget me not bears. Worldwide mailorder.

Sixpenny Bears
of Hawkshead

Bears from Around the World
in the heart of the Lake District

Usually over 600 Bears in stock
from over 50 makers

Come and see our own unique bears
and memoribilia

Buy Online at www. sixpennybears.com

All Bear Lovers
Welcome!

Visit our unique Bear shop &
get 10 % discount with this advert
The Square, Hawkshead, Cumbria

Tel: 015394 36003   Email: janine@sixpennybears.com

TEDDY BEARSVILLE

28 High Street, Rowley Regis, West Midlands, B65 0DR
☎ 0121 559 9990 Fax: As tel.
email: sales@teddybearsville.net
web: www.teddybearsville.net
Open 10-5.30, closed Thursday. Wide range including Steiff, Dean's, Teddy Hermann, Kosen, Clemens, Robin Rive. Layaway service. Mail order.

TEDDY LANE

☎ 01636 816017
email: customerservices@teddylane.co.uk
web: www.teddylane.co.uk
Teddy Lane specialises in the online sale of teddy bears, gift wrapped and delivered to friends and loved ones.

TEDDY'S ROOM

Haydnstr 8, D75045 Walzbachtal, Germany
☎ +49 162 4321132
email: bears@teddysroom.com
web: www.teddysroom.com
Watch Strap Bears - our own design. Specialists in miniature artist bears, limited editions and exclusives from all over the world.

TEDDYMILL

email: teddymill@hotmail.com
web: www.teddymill.co.uk
Leading UK suppliers of Bear Factory and Bear Mill teddies, outfits and party kits. Free UK delivery.

THOUGHTS

12 Trentham Retail Village, Trentham, Stoke-on-Trent, Staffordshire, ST4 8AX also at 62 High St, Stone, Staffs.
☎ 01782 641919
email: mike.dillon@btinternet.com
web: www.trentham.co.uk
Trentham is open 7 days a week. Stocking Steiff and Charlie Bears (some limited editions). Also Russ Berrie.

TOTO'S

5 Grafton Street, Altrincham, Cheshire, WA14 1DU
☎ 0161 928 7657 Fax: 0161 926 9693
email: info@totos.co.uk
web: www.totos.co.uk
Steiff Club Store. Full ecommerce website or visit us at our shop in Altrincham.

The Steiff Gallery

STEIFF GALLERY

The No1 store
for all your Steiff
The U.Ks most complete
range with many Exclusives,
special events and club
member offers.

The STEIFF Gallery
The Glades
Bromley, Kent
BR1 1DN
Tel. 0208 466 8444

www.steiff-gallery.co.uk
london@steiff-gallery.co.uk

THE TOY CHEST

1-2 Devonshire Arcade, Penrith, Cumbria, CA11 7SX
and 24 Lake Rd, Keswick.
☎ 01768 891237 / 017687 74953
web: www.toychestpenrith.co.uk
Largest collection of bears in Cumbria and the Lake District. Two shops Penrith and Keswick. Not to be missed.

TOY EMPORIUM

79 High Street, Bridgnorth, Shropshire, WV16 4DS
☎ 01746 765134 Fax: As tel.
email: THETOYEMP@aol.com
web: www.thetoyemporium.co.uk
Steiff Club, Hermann, Dean's, Merrythought.

TOY GALLERY

17 Ladygate, Beverley, East Yorkshire, HU17 8BH
☎ 01482 864890
email: enquiries@toygalleryuk.karoo.co.uk
web: www.toygalleryuk.com
Large selection of fabulous bears.

TRADITIONAL TOYS LTD

6 Bull Ring, Llantrisant, Mid-Glamorgan, CF72 8EB
☎ 01443 222693 Fax: 01443 238436
A Victorian shop offering a large range of teddy bears as well as hand-made wooden toys and rocking horses.

TREASURED TEDDIES

at Farnborough Garden Centre, Southam Road,
Farnborough, Banbury, Oxfordshire, OX17 1EL
☎ 01295 690479
The teddy lover's garden centre. Treasured gifts for every occasion. Cuddly collectables and furry friends.

URCHINS THE BEAR SHOP

The Old Mill, Boscastle Harbour, Boscastle, Cornwall,
PL35 0AQ
☎ 01840 250800
email: info@urchinsbears.com
web: www.urchinsbears.com
Steiff, Robin Rive, Baren & Bastel, Deb Canham, Charlie Bears Best Friends Store. Layaway & worldwide dispatch service available. Open all year!

CUMBRIA

Collectors Teddy Bears
Soft Toys & Fine Gifts

1-2 Devonshire Arcade, Penrith,
Cumbria. Tel: (01768) 891237

and

24 Lake Road, Keswick
Tel: (017687) 74953

www.toychestpenrith.co.uk

🐻 VILLAGE BEARS
2890 Hyde Park Street, Sarasota, Florida 34239, USA
☎ +1 941 366 2667 Fax: +1 941 366 0334
email: villagebears@att.net
web: www.villagebears.com
Specializing in R.John Wright, Steiff, Artist Bears, VanderBears, Golliwogs and Deb Canham. Worldwide shipping. Closed weekends and Mondays. Call for appointments.

● WELLFIELDS
Unit 7, The Globe Centre, Wellfield Road, Cardiff, South Glamorgan, CF24 3PE
☎ **02920 453045**
email: **wellfield.bears@ntlworld.com**
web: **www.wellfieldbears.co.uk**
Established teddy bear specialist and Steiff dealer. On site teddy bear repairs.

● WESTMEAD TEDDIES
The Tuck Shop, High Street, Godshill, Ventnor, Isle of Wight, PO38 3HH
☎ 01983 840643
Godshill's old tuck shop is home to teddies to suit all pockets from exclusive artist bears to pocket money teds.

We are located at the heart of the picturesque
market town of Beverley, East Riding of
Yorkshire, in a Georgian grade II listed building

We stock all your favourite Teddy Bears!

Steiff, Teddy Hermann, Steiner, Robin Rive, Dean's, Merrythought, Gund, Clemens,
Russ Berrie, Deb Canham, Cotswold Bears, Cliff Richard Collection, Hildegard Gunzel,
World of Miniatures, Dormouse, Mister bears and various Artist bears.

In addition you can browse our beautiful range of traditional wooden
toys and games, reminisce over the classic metal pedal cars and
then relax in our walled courtyard garden while you decide which of
our lovable Teddy Bears will be joining your family.

Please visit our website to learn more about Beverley, view our store,
browse our range and shop in the comfort of your own home.

www.toygalleryuk.com

Tel: 01482 864890 email: enquiries@toygalleryuk.karoo.co.uk
17 Ladygate, Beverley, East Yorks, HU17 8BH

● WOOKEY BEARS

Wookey Hole Caves, Wookey Hole, Wells, Somerset, BA5 1BB

☎ 01749 672243

web: www.wookey.co.uk

World famous bears to world famous caves and much more. Home to the British Bear Collection and many other bears.

● WORLD OF BEARS

20 Lower Middle Street, Taunton, Somerset, TA1 1SF

☎ 01823 332050

email: headbear@bear-world.com

web: www.worldofbears.com

Secure on-line ordering. When you have tried the best, why bother with the rest. Please see advert on page 25.

END

Shops and Sources for Old Bears

Welcome to this section on sources for old bears. Many are dealers who operate on an appointment basis or sell through fairs and the internet. Some have shops, and auction houses are also included.

The numbers of old bears held in stock may range from under ten to over 100. Readers are advised to telephone regarding stock and viewing arrangements before travelling a distance.

Picture courtesy of the
Puppenhausmuseum
in Basel, Switzerland.
See ad page 81

● ABBEY BEARS
11 The Market, Padstow, Cornwall, PL28 8AL
☎ 01841 532484
email: abbeybears@hotmail.co.uk
For old bears and animals.

● ALL YOU CAN BEAR
Stand A25-B15, Grays Mews Antique Market, Davies Mews, London, W1 2LD
☎ 020 8368 5491 Fax: 020 8368 5776
email: sarah@allyoucanbear.com
web: www.allyoucanbear.com
Specialising in vintage/artist bears.

● THE BEAR HUGGERY
Tower House, Castle Street, Douglas, Isle of Man, IM1 2EZ
☎ 01624 676333
email: bearhuggery@manx.net
web: www.thebearhuggery.co.uk
Genteel bearfolk awaiting suitable accommodation - references may be required. Sympathetic preservation undertaken for ailing bears. Artist, manufacturers, exclusives also available.

● THE BEAR PATCH
33 Market Place, Ashbourne, Derbyshire, DE6 1EU
☎ 01335 342391
web: www.thebearpatch.co.uk
Manufactured, artist and old bears.

● BEARNONI BEARS
Diane Walton, (near Johannesburg Airport), South
Africa
☎ +27 (0)11 849 1825
email: jesmond@iafrica.com
*Collector/dealer in old bears incl. Steiff, Bing,
Farnell, Cramer, Schuco etc. Also retired
White Label Steiff and bear memorabilia.*

● BEARS OF WINDY HILL
PO Box 51, Shipley, West Yorkshire, BD18 2YH
☎ 01274 599175 Fax: As tel.
email: info@bearsofwindyhill.co.uk
web: www.bearsofwindyhill.co.uk
Old bears, animals and dolls.

● BEBES ET JOUETS
☎ 01289 304802
email: bebesetjouets@tiscali.co.uk
web: coming soon!
*Finest antique teddies and dolls. Large
selection. Genuine old bears, no repros.
Photos available. Email or telephone for
friendly assistance.*

● BEE ANTIQUES AND COLLECTABLES
23B Albion Street, Broadstairs, Kent, CT10 1LU
☎ 01843 864040
email: theteddymaster@aol.com
web: www.bbears.co.uk
*Teddy hospital. Friendly personal service.
Free advice. Valuations. Swaps. Old Bears.
Visit our shop.*

● BONHAMS
Montpelier Street, Knightsbridge, London, SW7 1HH
☎ 08700 273627
email: rachel.gotch@bonhams.com
web: www.bonhams.com/toys
Auctioneers and valuers since 1793.

Bourton Bears
Give an old bear a home

See website for   Fair Dates

Antique and vintage bear specialists
Telephone 01452 760186
www.bourtonbears.com

When contacting advertisers please mention you saw their advertisement in the UK Teddy Bear Guide

Hugglets PUBLISHING

● GRANNY'S GOODIES

Unit 3, 34a Camden Passage/Islington Green, London, N1 8DU

☎ 020 8693 5432 or 020 7704 2210 (shop)

Fax: 020 8693 5432

email: klaregerwat-clark@tinyworld.co.uk

web: www.grannysgoodiesfairs.com

Antique & artist bears. Brenda Gerwat-Clark. Open Wednesday and Saturday only. 8.30 - 4.00. Also teddy bear hospital.

● GROWLERS TEDDY BEARS

35 Moorfield Road, Exmouth, Devon, EX8 3QN

☎ 01392 276891

email: soorimmer@btinternet.com

web: www.growlers-teddybears.co.uk

Growlers teddybears, the first teddy dating service. Find your perfect partner from the many mature single bears featured. Have fun!

● LEANDA HARWOOD
☎ 01529 300737
email: leanda.harwood@virgin.net
A large selection of good quality vintage bears and soft toys always in stock. See us at Hugglets Festivals.

● JEANNETTE - TEDDIES GALORE
☎ 0208 958 6101
email: amaz120@aol.com
web: www.jeannetteteddiesgalore.co.uk
Early Steiff, rare interesting bears, toys and accessories.

● MARTIN KIDMAN
Ditchling, East Sussex, BN6 8UR
☎ 01273 842938
email: info@martinkidman.com
web: www.martinkidman.com
Please see our display advertisement.

LUCKY BEARS LIMITED

PO Box 2064, Hockley, Essex, SS5 5YB
☎ 01702 204182 Fax: 0870 705 3249
email: enquiries@luckybears.com
web: www.luckybears.com
Antique, vintage and collectable bears

MARIGOLD BEARS

92 Wychwood Avenue, Knowle, Solihull, West Midlands, B93 9DQ
☎ 01564 776092
email: susancane@tiscali.co.uk
Vintage bears and other characters ready for happy new homes. They have been 'rescued', sometimes sympathetically restored, and always cleaned.

MARY SHORTLE

9 Lord Mayors Walk, York, North Yorkshire, also at 5 Bootham, York and 9, 15 & 17 Queen's Arcade, Leeds.
☎ 01904 425168 / 631165 / 634045; Tel: 01132 456160 (Leeds) Fax: 01904 425168
email: mary@maryshortleofyork.com
web: www.maryshortleofyork.com
Antique and modern teddies. Limited editions, miniature teddies, leading artists. Teddy bear hospital. Hundreds of teddies to choose from.

THE OLD BEAR COMPANY LTD

PO Box 29, Chesterfield, Derbyshire, S42 6ZE
☎ 01246 862387 Fax: 01246 863011
email: oldbears@oldbear.co.uk
web: www.oldbearcompany.com
Old teddies - please see display advertisement.

OLD BEARS NETWORK

Brown Cow Cottage, Godly Lane, Rishworth, Sowerby Bridge, West Yorkshire, HX6 4QR
☎ 01422 823079 Fax: As tel.
email: oldbears.network@zen.co.uk
web: www.oldbearsnetwork.co.uk
Vintage bears, clothing and accessories.

OLD PALACE ANTIQUES

Quay Street, Lostwithiel, Cornwall, PL22 0BS
☎ 01208 872909
email: melaniej.askew@virgin.net
web: www.old-palace-antiques.com
We buy and sell antique, vintage and collectable bears and dolls, clothing and accessories. Open Monday-Saturday 9.30am to 5.00pm.

OLD TIME BEARS

Ramsgate, Kent
☎ 01843 593619
email: info@oldtimebears.com
web: www.oldtimebears.com
Wide selection of antique vintage collectable teddy bears, animals and toys including Steiff, Merrythought, Chad Valley, Chiltern and lots more!

OLDBEARSCENE

☎ 01892 521232 / 07949 912292
Fax: 01892 521232
email: oldbearscene@yahoo.co.uk
web: www.oldbearscene.com
Antique bears, clothing and accessories.

SUE PEARSON

18 Brighton Square, The Lanes, Brighton, East Sussex, BN1 1HD
☎ 01273 774851/329247
email: sales@suepearson.co.uk
web: www.sue-pearson.co.uk
Please see advertisement page 5.

PEBBLE BEACH BEARS

☎ **01273 277747**
email: **jntfor@aol.com**
web: **www.pebblebeachbears.co.uk**
A wide selection of vintage teddy bears, animals and accessories for sale plus a few surprises.

PEEK-A-BOO TEDDY BEARS

Kent
☎ 020 8855 4499
email: sales@peekabooteddybears.co.uk
web: www.peekabooteddybears.co.uk
Specialising in Steiff limited editions.

PONGO'S BEARS

☎ 07952 578224
email: pongo@pongosbears.co.uk
web: www.pongosbears.co.uk
Purveying antique and vintage bears.

RAINEY DAYS OLD BEARS & FRIENDS

Lorraine Day
☎ 020 8647 6235
email: rainey@rainey-days.com
web: www.rainey-days.com
Rare and unusual teddies/friends.

SAD PAD BEARS

☎ 01622 754441
web: www.sadpadbears.com
Specialists in vintage Teddy Bears and classic soft toys. Restoration and hand cleaning.

● TEDDIES AND CHUMS

Leighton Buzzard, Bedfordshire
☎ 01525 635372 mob: 07969 811875
email: enquiries@teddiesandchums.co.uk
web: www.teddiesandchums.co.uk
Vintage bears, dogs, cats and other animals, books, clothing and accessories from early 1900's to 1960's.

● TEDDIES OF TRENODE

Higher Trenode Cottage, Widegates, Nr Looe, Cornwall, PL13 1QA
☎ 01503 240462 Fax: As tel.
email: enquiries@teddiesoftrenode.co.uk
web: www.teddiesoftrenode.co.uk
Tricia's Teddies of Trenode - specialists in old, antique, veteran and vintage teddies by world wide manufacturers.

● THE TEDDY BEAR CHEST

Pine Cottage, OX39 4RU
☎ **07913 872721**
email: vicky@theteddybearchest.co.uk
web: www.theteddybearchest.co.uk
The Teddy Bear Chest is home to a wide selection of vintage teddy bears dating from 1902 to 1940.

● TEDDY BEARS HOME

65 Sarratt Avenue, Hemel Hempstead, Hertfordshire, HP2 7JF
☎ 01442 267328
email: info@teddybearshome.com
web: www.teddybearshome.com
Specialists in collectable teddy bears.

● TEDDY BEARS OF WITNEY

99 High Street, Witney, Oxfordshire, OX28 6HY
☎ 01993 706616 Fax: 01993 702344
email: alfonzo@witneybears.co.uk
web: www.teddybears.co.uk
We pay fair prices for old teddy bears. We sell old bears in the shop, but not by mail order.

● THE TOY AUCTIONEER

Daniel Agnew
☎ 020 7870 8124
email: daniel@thetoyauctioneer.com
web: www.thetoyauctioneer.com
Please contact us for valuations and to sell your antique and vintage teddy bears and other collectable toys.

● TOYS OF YOUTH

PO Box 307, Bedford, Bedfordshire, MK43 8ZF
☎ 01234 841649 Fax: As tel.
email: info@toysofyouth.co.uk
web: www.toysofyouth.co.uk
Old bears and old toys for sale from our website, by mail order and at all major fairs. Bears purchased.

● VECTIS AUCTIONS

Fleck Way, Thornaby, Stockton-on-Tees, Cleveland, TS17 9JZ
☎ 01642 750616 Fax: 01642 769478
email: admin@vectis.co.uk
web: www.vectis.co.uk
Largest toy auctioneer in world.

● WOODEN HILL BEARS

Bath, Somerset
☎ 01225 442615
email: info@woodenhillbears.co.uk
web: www.woodenhillbears.co.uk
We hold an interesting selection of antique and vintage teddy bears, animals and accessories. New website planned for February 2008.

END

When calling a UK number from overseas please dial your international call code, then the country code of 44, then the UK number but omitting the first '0'

eg. the Hugglets number 01273 697974 would become +44 1273 697974

Teddy Bear Trail (shops index)

The Teddy Bear Trail has been compiled from the entries in our shops and sources sections which we understand to be retail outlets open during normal shop hours. Some are specialist teddy bear shops while others are general toy and gift shops which sell teddy bears. Please check opening times and stock details etc, before travelling a distance. See main listing in the shops section for more information. For your convenience, entries have been grouped into areas (see map below).

The codes which appear after the name of the business refer to the number of makers and different designs which you might expect to find there.

We asked the shops to indicate the bands they fall within. Our questions and the key for the codes appear below.

Question 1: How many different makers (bear artists or manufacturers) do you normally stock?
A) 1-10   B) 11-25   C) 26-50   D) 51-100   E) over 100

Question 2 How many different designs/models of teddy bear do you normally have in stock?
F) 1-25   G) 26-100)   H) 101-250   I) over 250

London & Southern Counties

Berkshire	Eton	Asquiths	E/I
Berkshire	Reading	Life Like Friends	B/I
East Sussex	Brighton	Pearson, Sue	E/I
Hampshire	Aldershot	Inspirations	A/F
Hampshire	Beaulieu	Bear It In Mind	B/H
Hampshire	Burley, Ringwood	Goldilocks	B/G
Hampshire	Ibsley	St Martin's Gallery	A/I
Hampshire	Lyndhurst	Paws in the Forest	B/G
Hampshire	Milford-on-Sea	Milford Models & Hobbies	B/H
Hampshire	Pamber End	Dolly Daydreams	B/F
Hampshire	Ringwood	Heavenly Creations	A/G

Hugglets PUBLISHING

Isle of Wight	Newport	Beavis, I C Ltd	A/G
Isle of Wight	Ryde	Koko's Bear Shop	B/I
Isle of Wight	Ventnor	Westmead Teddies	C/I
Kent	Broadstairs	Bee Antiques and Collectables	B/G
Kent	Bromley	Steiff Gallery	A/I
Kent	Faversham	Arctophilia	C/I
Kent	Maidstone	Oyster Box, The	A/G
Kent	Tonbridge	Greta May	B/G
London	London	Dolly Land	C/I
London	London	Granny's Goodies	C/H
London	London	Hamleys of London	D/I
Surrey	Guildford	Bear Garden, The	D/I
West Sussex	Lindfield	Kieron James Designs	B/H

Central England

Bedfordshire	Bedford	Beavis, C J Ltd	A/G
Buckinghamshire	Little Marlow	Bucks Bears	B/I
Derbyshire	Ashbourne	Bear Patch, The	C/I
Derbyshire	Bakewell	Ce Gifts & Bears	B/H
Derbyshire	Hope Valley	Causeway Crafts/Cinnamon Bear	A/G
Derbyshire	Ridgeway, Nr Sheffield	Bear Emporium, The	B/H
Derbyshire	Ridgeway, Nr Sheffield	Bear Emporium, The	B/H
Gloucestershire	Cheltenham	Pied Piper, The	C/I
Herefordshire	Ledbury	Apple Pie House Ltd	B/I
Leicestershire	Ashby-de-la Zouch	Ashby Bears & Collectables	B/I
Nottinghamshire	Newark	Gift, The	A/I
Oxfordshire	Farnborough, Banbury	Treasured Teddies	B/H
Oxfordshire	Witney	Teddy Bears of Witney	E/I
Shropshire	Ironbridge	Bears on the Square	E/I
Shropshire	Ludlow	Little Paws	B/G
Warwickshire	Coventry	Cejais Bears & Dollshouses	A/H
Warwickshire	Stratford upon Avon	Curtis Brae of Stratford	B/I
West Midlands	Kingswinford	Ashwood Nurseries Gift Shop	A/H
West Midlands	Rowley Regis	Teddy Bearsville	B/H
West Midlands	Wombourne	Let's Go Round Again	A/G

The West Country

Avon	Bath	Party Bears	B/G
Avon	Bristol	Carol's Tiny Treasures	C/H
Avon	Bristol	Razzle Dazzle	D/H
Cornwall	Boscastle	Urchins The Bear Shop	B/H
Cornwall	East Looe	Abbey Bears	B/I
Cornwall	Padstow	Abbey Bears	B/I
Devon	Dartmouth	Kingswear Bears and Friends	B/I
Devon	Torquay	Halcyon of St. Marychurch	A/G
Dorset	Dorchester	Teddy Bear House	C/I
Somerset	Cheddar Gorge	Gorge Bear Company	D/I
Somerset	Taunton	World of Bears	D/I
Somerset	Wells	Wookey Bears	C/I

Wales

Mid-Glamorgan	Llantrisant	Traditional Toys Ltd	B/I

Scotland

Ross-shire	Invergordon	Cuddly Kerrlectables	B/I
Tayside	Broughty Ferry, Dundee	Broughty Bears	A/G

Eastern Counties

Cambridgeshire	Cambridge	Parade - The Gift Shop	A/F
Cambridgeshire	Huntingdon	Bears To Collect	B/I
Essex	Colchester	Bear Shop, Colchester, The	D/I
Essex	Leigh-on-Sea	Leigh Toy Fair	B/H
Essex	Saffron Walden	Abracadabra Teddy Bears	D/I
Lincolnshire	Bourne	Teddy Bears & Friends of Bourne	C/I
Norfolk	Cromer	Allsorts of bears	C/I
Norfolk	Norwich	Bear Shop, Norwich, The	D/I
North Lincolnshire	Barton-upon-Humber	Daisa Original Designs Ltd	A/F
Suffolk	Bacton, Stowmarket	Bacton Bears	A/I
Suffolk	Woodbridge	Bears & Stitches	A/G
Cheshire	Altrincham	Toto's	A/H
Cheshire	Sandiway	Cobblestone Bears and Gifts	C/H

The North

Cumbria	Hawkshead	Sixpenny Bears	C/I
Cumbria	Penrith	Toy Chest, The	B/I
East Yorkshire	Beverley	Toy Gallery	B/H
Isle of Man	Douglas	Bear Huggery, The	D/I
Lancashire	Wigan	Bears 'n' Things	B/G
North Yorkshire	Leyburn	Hartley's of Leyburn	
North Yorkshire	Scarborough	Bar Street Bears	C/H
North Yorkshire	York	Christmas Angels	C/I
North Yorkshire	York	Mary Shortle	E/I
South Yorkshire	Rotherham	Bears Den, The	C/I
Tyne & Wear	South Shields	Dolly Domain of South Shields	B/I
West Yorkshire	Halifax	Serendipity	B/H
West Yorkshire	Sowerby Bridge	Memory Lane	A/I

END

Bear Making Supplies & Courses

The products on offer by any individual or company are listed in the belief that they are suitable for bearmaking.

However, no responsibility can be accepted by the publisher and readers must satisfy themselves on all matters regarding safety.

● ADMIRAL BEARS SUPPLIES

16 Ormonde Avenue, Epsom, Surrey, KT19 9EP
☎ 01372 813558 Fax: As tel.
email: netty.paterson@ntlworld.com
web: www.admiral-bears.com
Suppliers of Schulte mohair, synthetics and other fabrics, mini bear supplies and also hand dyed mohairs & synthetics - see display advertisement.

● BEAR BASICS

Unit 2 Marsh View, Marsh Lane, Henstridge Trading Estate, Henstridge, Somerset, BA8 0TG
☎ 01963 364777
email: enquiries@bearbasics.co.uk
web: www.bearbasics.co.uk
We supply bear makers in the UK and around the world. For all your bear making needs. See our display advert.

● THE BEAR SUPPLIES COMPANY

@ Wylde About Bears, 'Four Seasons', Hall Lane, West Rainton, Co. Durham, DH4 6PF
☎ 0191 584 1111 / 07835 712888
email: wyldeaboutbears@hotmail.com
web: www.bearsupplies.co.uk
Everything you need to make that special Bear. Mohair, joints, eyes, fillings and much much more. Courses also available.

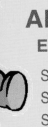

THE BEARS DEN

Craft Corner, 6 Riverside Precinct, Corporation Street, Rotherham, South Yorkshire, S60 1ND
☎ 01709 828619
email: thebearsden@topliss123.fsnet.co.uk
Mohair and bear making supplies.

BEARY CHEAP BEAR SUPPLIES

PO Box 2465, Burleigh, Queensland 4220, Australia
☎ +61 (0)7 5520 3455 Fax: +61 (0)7 5520 3411
email: sales@bearycheap.com
web: www.bearycheap.com
The web's largest range of on-line Teddy Bear Making Supplies. Mohair, synthetic fur & lots more. Worldwide mail order service.

BEARY SPECIAL SUPPLIES

Woodland Teddies, 5 Mildenhall Road, Loughborough, Leicestershire, LE11 4SN
☎ 01509 267597 mob: 07973 821816
email: supplies@woodlandteddies.com
web: www.woodlandteddies.co.uk
From colourful mohair dyes and ultrasuede to needlefelting supplies we offer everything to make teddies special including work-shops. See display.

Roy and Pat would like to thank all of their Oakley Fabrics customers for their valued support over the past 30 years.

February 2007 saw their retirement and handover of Oakley Fabrics to Susan of Bear Basics. Ensuring a continuation of the UK's direct partnership with Reinhardt Schulte obtaining mohair directly from the mill and meeting all your bear making needs.

The warehouse in Luton is now closed. For all enquiries please contact Bear Basics directly, see their advert for contact details.

Bear Basics

BEDDINGFIELD BEARS

80 Beaumont Walk, Leicester, LE4 0PQ
☎ 0796 3723220
email: beddingfieldbears@btinternet.com
web: www.beddingfieldbears.co.uk
Mohair at bargain prices. Off cuts always available at low prices. Fast and low priced delivery.

CALICO PIE

305 Lancaster Road, Morecambe, Lancashire, LA4 5TP
☎ 01524 412460 Fax: As tel.
email: carol@calicopie.co.uk
web: www.calicopie.co.uk
Mail order craft supplies.

CHRISTIE BEARS LIMITED

Ref GD02, The Mount, Clevis Hill, Newton, Porthcawl, CF36 5NT
☎ 01656 789054 Fax: 01656 785044
email: enquiries@christiebears.co.uk
web: www.christiebears.co.uk
Suppliers of fabrics, components and tools to teddy bear makers around the world.

COURSES WITH BEAR BITS

The Florins, Silver Street, Minting, Horncastle, Lincolnshire, LN9 5RP
☎ 01507 578360 Fax: As tel.
email: ashburner@bearbits.freeserve.co.uk
web: www.bearbits.com
Exclusive weekend bear making courses for beginners, improvers or advanced addicts! Very small numbers only. For information please send SAE.

CUDDY LUGS

16 Hays Close, Willersey, Broadway, Worcestershire, WR12 7QA
☎ 01386 858134
email: sheila@cuddylugs.com
web: www.cuddylugs.com
Knitting patterns for bears and dolls clothes. Yarn packs, needles. Send £3 for big cata-logue or shop on line.

"Create teddy bear magic from our bear basics!"

Proudly presenting a new and rapidly expanding range of fabulous mohair
and alpaca fabrics from the world famous Schulte mill.
Along with English glass eyes in a range of fabulous colours, wonderful paw
fabrics, joints, threads, fabric pens, growlers and tools.
Patterns and kits are available too.
Mix together and create your own teddy magic!

Domino
by
Anita Weller

Bear
Basics

Fudge
by
Catherine Young

Now incorporating Oakley Fabrics

www.bearbasics.co.uk

We shall be introducing exciting new patterns in our two new series:
"The Best of British" and "Around the World".

Featuring some familiar and well established names and some new exciting stars!!

The new Exclusive Official Authorised Partner for Schulte Mohair within the UK

Tel (+44) 01963 364777   Monday – Friday 10am – 4pm
Visit us by appointment at
Unit 2 Marsh View, Marsh Lane, Henstridge Trading Estate,
Henstridge, Somerset, BA8 0TG.
Email: enquiries@bearbasics.co.uk

DOLLS DESIGNS

Jane Woodbridge, 6 Newmans Gardens, Sompting, Lancing, West Sussex, BN15 0BD
☎ 01903 602988
email: dollywood@ntlworld.com
Knitting patterns for dolls and some teddies, 76 designs, eleven knitting books for dolls, plus fine yarns and knitting needles.

EMMARY BEARS

'Ridgeway', Bodmin Hill, Lostwithiel, Cornwall, PL22 0AJ
☎ 01208 872251
web: www.emmarybears.co.uk
A large and varied selection of hand dyed mohair, components, patterns, kits and accessories. Wholesale rates also available.

G & T EVANS WOODWOOL

Dulas Mill, Ffordd Mochdre, Newtown, Powys, SY16 4JD
☎ 01686 622100 Fax: 01686 622220
email: gtevans1@aol.com
web: www.gtevans.co.uk
Manufacturers of superfine grades of wood wool. Samples available. For full details and list of stockists, call us today.

THE GLASS EYE CO.

School Bank Road, Llanrwst, Gwynedd, LL26 0HU
☎ 01492 642220 Fax: 01492 641643
email: enquiries@stsnorthwales.co.uk
web: www.glasseyes.com
FREE! Full colour wall chart.

HAND GLASS CRAFT

105 Dudley Road, Brierley Hill, West Midlands, DY5 1HD
☎ 01384 573410 Fax: 01384 486467
web: www.handglasscraft.com
Please see display advertisement.

A HELMBOLD GMBH

Plüschweberei und Färberei, Hauptstr. 44, D-98634, Oberweid, Germany
☎ +49 (0)36946 22009 Fax: +49 (0)36946 22020
email: Helmbold_GmbH@t-online.de
web: www.A-Helmbold.de
Please see display advertisement.

Toy Plush

since 1900

Traditional manufacturer of toy plush made from **mohair, wool, alpaca, cotton and artificial silk.**

International despatch service.

Further information from:

A. Helmbold GmbH
Plüschweberei und Färberei
D-98634 Oberweid, Hauptstraße 44
Tel: +49 36946-22009
Fax: +49 36946-22020
email: Helmbold_GmbH@t-online.de
web: www.A-Helmbold.de

When contacting advertisers
please mention you saw their advertisement in the **UK Teddy Bear Guide 2008**

REINHOLD LESCH GMBH

Ursula Clements, UK agent, Garden Flat, 4 Strathray Gardens, London, NW3 4NY

☎ 020 7794 2377 Fax: 020 7209 4799

email: ugmclements@yahoo.co.uk

German manufacturers of bear making components - quality glass and safety eyes, growlers, joints, etc. - catalogue available on request.

LYNDA BROWN BEARS

18 Sutton Way, Hounslow, Middlesex, TW5 0JA

☎ 020 8570 0095

Small selection of mohair and Fiskars scissors. Please send sae or telephone for information.

LYRICAL BEARS

26 Cromwell Road, Stevenage, Hertfordshire, SG2 9HT

☎ 01438 351651 Fax: As tel.

email: info@lyrical-bears.co.uk

web: www.lyrical-bears.co.uk

Miniature bear making supplies, kits, fabrics, eyes, joints etc. Biggest range in the UK. Please note our new address.

NEW FOREST BEARS

9 Chy Pons, St Austell, Cornwall, PL25 5DH

☎ 01726 76505

email: gilbears@aol.com

Beginners'/advanced bear making and design workshops. Miniatures a speciality. Please send sae for details.

NORBEARY FABRICS

42 Palmarsh Avenue, Hythe, Kent, CT21 6NR

☎ 01303 269038 Fax: 01303 266669

email: barbaraannbears@msn.com

web: www.norbearyfabrics.co.uk

Mohair! Huge range offering great value, suitable for vintage, traditional, modern and crazy style bears. Schulte stockist. Samples (75+) £10.

Sew What & Stuff It
Bear making supplies from Tracey James

All the tools of the trade: eyes, joints,
threads, fillings, paw material,
over 100 types of Mohair & Alpaca.
Miniature Bear Supplies.

Please telephone (01925) 725084

or check website for a list of fair dates and venues.

Major credit cards accepted. Mail order service available.

enquiries@sewwhatandstuffit.co.uk

www.sewwhatandstuffit.co.uk

Woodland Teddies
Beary Special Supplies
(& furries)

Beautiful furries &
everything to make
your creations special
• Rainbow dyes
• Handpainted eyes
• Colourful ultrasuede
• Original Patterns & kits • Fillers
• Needlefelting supplies • Noses
• Dyeing service • Hand Dyed Mohair
• 1 to 1 tuition & specialist workshops
Furries: www.woodlandteddies.com
Supplies: www.woodlandteddies.co.uk
5 Mildenhall Road, LE11 4SN +44 (0)1509 267597
email supplies@woodlandteddies.com

● PEACOCK FIBRES LTD
Gain Mill, Gain Lane, Bradford, West Yorkshire,
BD2 3LW
☎ 01274 633900 Fax: 01274 633910
email: info@noblecraft.co.uk
web: www.noblecraft.co.uk
*English mohair, ultrasuede, polyester fillings
(regular, heavy, super, lux). Recycled fibre,
kapok, woodwool, shot, tendertouch baby
fat. Next day delivery.*

● PROBÄR GMBH
Heinrich Hertz Str 9, D48599 Gronau, Germany
☎ +49 (0)2562 7013 0 Fax: +49 (0)2562 7013 33
email: info@probear.com
web: www.probear.com
Please see display advertisement.

● SEW WHAT & STUFF IT BEAR MAKING SUPPLIES
Cheshire
☎ 01925 725084
email: enquiries@sewwhatandstuffit.co.uk
web: www.sewwhatandstuffit.co.uk
Please see display advertisement.

● TEDDYTECH
49 Florida Road, Durban 4001, Kwa Zulu Natal, South
Africa
☎ +27 (0)31 312 7755 Fax: +27 (0)31 312 9564
email: ebeaton@global.co.za
web: www.teddytech.biz
*Where the magic of bearmaking begins.
Importers and distributors of Schulte mohair,
suppliers of artist designed kits & related
bearmaking supplies.*

● THREADTEDS
De Braak 11, 5963 BA Horst, Netherlands
☎ +31 (0)77 3984960
email: threadteds@xs4all.nl
web: www.threadteds.com
*Original traditional, crochet, needle felted
and crofelt artist collectables. Offering thread
bear patterns, book, kits, mini fabric and supplies!*

END

The largest supplier of "Schulte" mohair worldwide.

PRO Bär GmbH

A part of the ProBear warehouse in Gronau.

4216 4210 4217 4211 4214 4213 4215 4212

Nico ± 23 cm

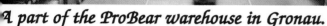

4210 4211 4212 4213
4214 4215 4216 4217

Medium dense, ± 8 mm straight pile € 74,00 per meter

In close cooperation with Schulte we have created two new series. A brandnew yarn with 70 % Mohair and 30 % artificial silk, this gives the fabric a very special silver, silky lustre.

4220 4221 4222 4223
4224 4225 4226 4227
4228

Medium dense, ± 24 mm
antique curly pile
€ 78,00 per meter

Bing-Bear ± 60 cm

4220

4214

Our distributors for the UK for our total fabric programme
Barbara-Ann Bears with Norbeary fabrics; Barbara-Ann Cunningham, Kent -
http://www.barbara-annbears.co.uk - Phone: 01303/269038
Jacqlynbears; Jacqulyn Ellerton, Leek Staffordshire -
http://www.jacqlynbears.com - Phone: 01538-388831

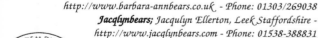

PROBÄR GmbH *
Heinrich-Hertz-Str. 9 * D 48599 Gronau *
Tel.: 0049 2562 7013-0 *
Fax: 0049 2562 7013-33 *
www.probear.com * info@probear.com

www.schulte-mohair.de
est. 1901
Reinhard Schulte GmbH

A list of the fair dates known at the time of publication can be found in the Fair Dates listing on page 72.

Dates can change so we recommend you confirm details with the organisers before travelling a distance.

● BOBBYS BEARS FAIRS

4 Station Road, Blackrod, Bolton, Lancashire, BL6 5BN
☎ 01204 697419 or 468090 Fax: 01204 695744
email: bobbys.bears@virgin.net
Bobbys Bears Fairs - the new organisers at Rivington Hall Barn. Please see display advertisement for 2008 details.

● BRITISH BEAR FAIR

Wendy's World, Pickwell Place, Cheapside Lane, Denham Village, Buckinghamshire, UB9 5AD
☎ 01895 834348
email: wendyhobday@freenet.co.uk
web: www.wendysworldfairs.co.uk
Sunday December 9th 2007. The British Bear Fair including the British Bear Artist Awards finals at Hove Town Hall, Sussex

● CORNWALL AND DEVON BEAR FAIRS

Organised by Emmary Fairs
☎ 01208 872251 Fax: As tel.
email: mary.saundry@btinternet.com
web: www.emmarybears.co.uk
Cornwall Bear Fairs (at Lostwithiel): 25th November 2007 and 22nd June 2008. Devon (at Exmouth): 18th May 2008. Over 45 stalls.

● DOLL & TEDDY FAIRS

Held at the National Motorcycle Museum
☎ 01530 274377 Fax: 024 7639 2284
email: debbie@woodhouse2364.fsnet.co.uk
Quality fairs with old, collectable, artist bears and dolls. See display advertisement.

● DOLLY'S DAYDREAMS

PO Box 1, Wisbech, Cambridgeshire, PE13 4QJ
☎ 01945 870160 Fax: 01945 870660
email: dollysdaydreams@supanet.com
web: www.dollysdaydreams.com
Kelham Hall, Kelham, near Newark, Nottinghamshire, NG23 5QX. Teddies, Dolls, Dolls Houses & Miniatures. Fair now in its 15th year!

● GRANNY'S GOODIES

PO Box 734, Forest Hill, London, SE23 2RQ
☎ 020 8693 5432 or 020 704 2210 Fax: 020 8693 5432
email: klaregerwat-clark@tinyworld.co.uk
web: www.grannysgoodiesfairs.com
Longest established Kensington fair organisers 1977 est. for teddy bear fairs. Largest selection of antique bears.

THE 3RD EUROPEAN TEDDY BEAR FAIR
APRIL 5th & 6th 2008

THE
GREAT
BEAR

ARPAILLARGUES - UZES
SOUTH OF FRANCE
Tel: 00.33.(0)4.66.57.25.13
www.jouetmusee.com

● LEEDS DOLL & TEDDY FAIR

Dolly Domain Fairs, 45 Henderson Road, South Shields, Tyne & Wear, NE34 9QW

☎ 0191 42 40 400 Fax: As tel.

email: fairs@dollydomain.com

web: www.dollydomain.com

Britain's oldest provincial teddy and doll fair. Twice yearly since 1982. FREE parking, see display advertisement for dates and details.

● TEDDIES 2008

Organisers: Hugglets, PO Box 290, Brighton, East Sussex, BN2 1DR

☎ **01273 697974 Fax: 01273 626255**

email: info@hugglets.co.uk

web: www.hugglets.co.uk

Sunday 14th September 2008 at Kensington Town Hall, London, W8 7NX. Britain's longest established teddy event, 170 stands. The original British Teddy Bear Festival. Thousands of bears, old and new, for sale. See website for exhibitor list and more information.

● TOTALLY TEDDIES

Sunnyside, Wyatts Green Road, Brentwood, Essex, CM15 0PT

☎ 01277 821890 Fax: 01277 822528

email: marsdraymo@aol.com

web: www.freewebs.com/totallyteddies

Now under new ownership. Jacqui and Ray Marsden invite you to attend the Totally Teddies fairs for 2007-2008.

● THE WINTER BEARFEST

Organisers: Hugglets, PO Box 290, Brighton, East Sussex, BN2 1DR

☎ **01273 697974 Fax: 01273 626255**

email: info@hugglets.co.uk

web: www.hugglets.co.uk

Sunday 24th February 2008 at Kensington Town Hall, Hornton Street, London, W8 7NX. 170 stands. Thousands of bears, old and new, for sale. See web site for exhibitor list and more information.

END

TOTALLY TEDDIES 2007/2008

Jacqui & Ray Marsden, Sunnyside,
Wyatts Green Road, Brentwood, Essex, CM15 0PT
Tel: 01277 821890 Fax 01277 822528
www.freewebs.com/totallyteddies email: marsdraymo@aol.com

RECOGNIZED THROUGHOUT THE TEDDY WORLD
THESE ARE SOME OF THE UK'S MOST FAMOUS FAIRS

The Hampshire Teddy Bear Fair

Sunday 18th November 2007
Sunday 11th May 2008 & Sunday 16th November 2008
BOTLEIGH GRANGE, Hedge End, Southampton

The Warwickshire Bear Fair

Sunday 17th February 2008
Stratford Holiday Inn, Bridgefoot,
Stratford-upon-Avon

The Rochester Teddy Bear Fair

Sundays 9th March 2008 & 5th October
FREE VALUATIONS ON BEARS & TOYS
BY BONHAM'S AUCTIONEERS
CORN EXCHANGE, ROCHESTER, KENT

TOTALLY TEDDIES

THE PROGRAMME

TOTALLY TEDDIES

THE WONDERFUL WORLD OF TEDDIES

UNDER NEW OWNERSHIP

2007

Harlow Park Inn	4th November 2007
Southampton Botleigh Grange	18th November 2007

New Season for 2008

Stratford Holiday Inn	17th February 2008
Southend Cliff Pavilion	2nd March 2008
Rochester Corn Exchange	9th March 2008
Novotel Hotel, Ipswich	6th April 2008
New venue to be announced	April 2008
Brentwood Holiday Inn	20th April 2008
Southampton Botleigh Grange	11th May 2008
New venue to be announced	May 2008
New venue to be announced	June 2008
Dorchester Maurward House	20th July 2008
Palms Hotel, Hornchurch, Essex	24th August 2008
Bracknell Leisure Centre	September 2008
Rochester Corn Exchange	5th October 2008
Harlow Park Inn Hotel	November date TBA
Southampton Botleigh Grange	16th November 2008

ALL FAIRS ARE CLEARLY SIGNPOSTED LOCALLY
WIN A LIMITED EDITION ARTIST TEDDY BEAR
there's a FREE PRIZE DRAW AT EACH FAIR

TOTALLY **TEDDIES**   01277 821890

PUBLISHING **Hugglets**

HUGGLETS

at Kensington Town Hall Hornton Street, London

Twice a year Hugglets Festivals offer you over 170 stands in four bear-packed halls. Choose from 10,000 bears and related collectables on sale at each event.

With 4 halls there's always something magical around the corner!

© Prue Theobalds

WINTER BEARFEST

Sunday 24th February 2008
(2009: Sunday 22nd February)

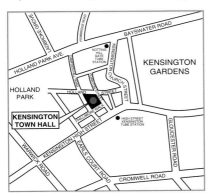

MID SEPTEMBER
TEDDIES 2008

Sunday 14th September 2008
(2009: Sunday 13th September)

Entry 11am - 4.30pm
Tickets at door: £4 adult, £2 child

Parking is only £4 for the day. 400 spaces.
Nearest Tube is High Street Kensington

Complimentary entry tickets on pages 191-193

Hugglets, PO Box 290, Brighton, BN2 1DR Tel: +44 (0)1273 697974
Fax: +44 (0)1273 62 62 55 Email: info@hugglets.co.uk www.hugglets.co.uk

See you there!

FESTIVALS
Hugglets

UK Bear Fair Dates

Key to Fair Organisers

BBB	Bobby's Bear Fairs	01204 468090	GG	Granny's Goodies		0208 693 5432
DD	Dolly's Daydreams	01945 870160	H	Hugglets		01273 697974
DDF	Dolly Domain Fairs	0191 424 0400	MJ	Musée du Jouet	+33 (0)4 66 57 25 13	
DTF	Doll & Teddy Fairs	01530 274377	TT	Totally Teddies		01277 821890
EF	Emmary Fairs	01208 872251	WW	Wendy's World		01895 834348

This listing gives details of all the fairs known to us at the time of publication at which teddy bears are for sale. Please note that many of the events are not exclusively for bears. The figure given after the venue specifies, where known, the approximate number of stands, but at non-exclusive shows these are not all teddy bears. Dates and venues can change, so we recommend you confirm details with the organisers before travelling a distance. The list has been compiled from information supplied by the organisers who are listed in the Guide.

November 2007

Sun	4th	Harlow Teddy Bear Festival, Park Inn Hotel, Harlow	70	TT
Sun	11th	The London International Antique Dolls, Toys, Miniatures & Teddy Bear Fair		
		Kensington Town Hall, Hornton Street, London		GG
Sun	18th	Hampshire Teddy Bear Festival		
		Botleigh Grange Hotel, Hedge End, Southampton	70	TT
Sun	25th	Vintage Bear, Doll & Toy Fair		
		National Motorcycle Museum, Bickenhill, Nr Birmingham	up to 90	DTF
Sun	25th	Cornwall Christmas Bear Fair		
		Lostwithiel Community Centre, Lostwithiel, Cornwall	45+	EF

December 2007

Sun	9th	The British Bear Fair 2007 Hove Town Hall, Norton Road, Hove	140	WW

January 2008

Sun	20th	The Kelham Hall Double, Kelham Hall, Kelham, Nr Newark, Notts	100	DD

February 2008

Sun	10th	The London International Antique Dolls, Toys, Miniatures & Teddy Bear Fair		
		Kensington Town Hall, Hornton Street, London		GG
Sun	17th	The Kelham Hall Double, Kelham Hall, Kelham, Nr Newark, Notts	100	DD
Sun	17th	Stratford-upon-Avon Teddy Bear Fair		
		Holiday Inn, Stratford Upon Avon	Up to 40	TT
Sun	24th	Winter BearFest 2008,		
		Kensington Town Hall, Hornton St, London, W8 7NX	170	H

Winter BearFest

Sunday 24th February 2008
Kensington Town Hall, Hornton Street, London
The exhibitor list for the Winter BearFest is available at www.hugglets.co.uk

March 2008

Sun	2nd	Southend Teddy Bear Fair, Cliff Pavilion, Southend	Up to 30	TT
Sat	8th	Bobby's Bear Fairs		
		Rivington Hall Barn (Jnc 6 M61), Horwich, Nr Bolton	55	BBB
Sun	9th	Rochester Teddy Bear FairCorn Exchange, Rochester	Up to 55	TT
Sun	23rd	The Great Spring Doll & Teddy Fair		
		National Motorcycle Museum, Bickenhill, Nr Birmingham	up to 90	DTF
Sat	29th	Leeds Doll & Teddy Fair		
		Pudsey Civic Hall, Pudsey, Leeds, LS28 5TA	85	DDF

April 2008

Sa/Su 5/6	The Great Bear, Musée du Jouet, Uzès, France		MJ
Sun 6th	Suffolk Bear Fair, Novotel Hotel, Ipswich	Up to 35	TT
Sun 13th	The London International Antique Dolls, Toys, Miniatures & Teddy Bear Fair		
	Kensington Town Hall, Hornton Street, London		GG
Sun 20th	Essex Bear Fair, Holiday Inn Hotel, Brentwood, J28 of M25	Up to 35	TT

May 2008

Sun	11th	Hampshire Teddy Bear Festival		
		Botleigh Grange Hotel, Hedge End, Southampton	50	TT
Sun	18th	Devon Bear Fair, Exmouth Pavilion, The Esplanade, Exmouth	45+	EF

June 2008

Sun 22nd Cornwall Bear Fair
                Lostwithiel Community Centre, Lostwithiel, Cornwall   45+   EF

July 2008

Sun 6th   The Kelham Hall Double, Kelham Hall, Kelham, Nr Newark, Notts   100   DD
Sun 20th Hampshire Teddy Bear Festival, Maurward House, Dorchester   50   TT

August 2008

Sun 24th Hornchurch Bear Fair, Palms Hotel, Hornchurch, Essex   up to 44   TT

September 2008

Sun 14th Teddies 2008, Kensington Town Hall, Hornton St, London, W8 7NX 170   H

FESTIVALS Hugglets — TEDDIES 2008

Sunday 14th September 2008
Kensington Town Hall, Hornton Street, London

The exhibitor list for Teddies 2008 is available at www.hugglets.co.uk

Sun 21st The London International Antique Dolls, Toys, Miniatures & Teddy Bear Fair
                Kensington Town Hall, Hornton Street, London   GG
Sun 28th Great Autumn Doll & Teddy Extravaganza
                National Motorcycle Museum, Bickenhill, Nr Birmingham   up to 90   DTF

October 2008

Sun 5th   Rochester Teddy Bear Fair, Corn Exchange, Rochester   Up to 55   TT
Sat 11th Leeds Doll & Teddy Fair
                Pudsey Civic Hall, Pudsey, Leeds, LS28 5TA   85   DDF
Sat 25th Bobby's Bear Fairs
                Rivington Hall Barn (Jnc 6 M61), Horwich, Nr Bolton   55   BBB

END

Bear Repairers

The following list of repairers is given in the belief that they are capable and experienced in their work. However, no responsibility is accepted for work carried out and readers must satisfy themselves on all such matters.

● ANGIEBEARS
27 Trubridge Road, Hoo St Werburgh, Rochester, Kent, ME3 9EN
☎ 01634 253165
email: angie@angiebears.net
web: www.angiebears.net
Repairer of old and antique bears, also a professional cleaning service is available.

● BA'S BEARS
5 Grove Street, Oxford, Oxfordshire, OX2 7JT
☎ 01865 435314
email: babruyn@hotmail.com
web: www.basbears.com
Sympathetic restoration and repairs.

● THE BEAR EMPORIUM
Well View, Ridgeway Craft Centre, Ridgeway, Nr Sheffield, Derbyshire, S12 3XR
☎ 01142 482010
web: www.bear-emporium.com
Plenty of love and care given to your special friend by expert restorers. No repair has defeated us yet.

● THE BEAR GARDEN
10 Jeffries Passage, Guildford, Surrey, GU1 4AP
☎ 01483 302581 Fax: 01483 457393
email: bears@beargarden.co.uk
web: www.beargarden.co.uk
Teddy bear and doll repairs.

● THE BEAR HUGGERY
Tower House, Castle Street, Douglas, Isle of Man, IM1 2EZ
☎ 01624 676333 email: bearhuggery@manx.net
web: www.thebearhuggery.co.uk
Sympathetic restoration of ailing bears in our Teddy Hospital, many years experience from simple cleaning to dog attacks. Quotes before treatment.

THE BEAR PATCH

33 Market Place, Ashbourne, Derbyshire, DE6 1EU
☎ 01335 342391
web: www.thebearpatch.co.uk
Well-loved bears expertly repaired by Pauline Johnson of Cubley Bears. Free quotation. Call at shop or phone for advice.

BEARS BY SUSAN JANE KNOCK

6 Elizabeth Avenue, Witham, Essex, CM8 1JE
☎ 01376 521230
email: susan.k@tinyworld.co.uk
Bear artist offers careful and sympathetic repairs for old and invalid bears and toys.

BORN AGAIN BEARS

Fareham, Hampshire
☎ 01329 313786 Fax: 01329 829875
email: sue@bornagainbears.co.uk
web: www.bornagainbears.co.uk
Exceptional quality restoration of treasured bears and soft toys. Highly recommended worldwide by Steiff, Harrods and top auctioneers. Postal service.

BRACKEN BEARS

Apple Loft, South Trigon, Wareham, Dorset, BH20 7PD
☎ 01929 554055 Fax: As tel.
Send your bears to our new hospital in Dorset's beautiful woodland countryside. They will return home refreshed, happy and healthy!

BRIAN'S BEAR HEART HOSPITAL

76 Shortwood Avenue, Staines, Middlesex, TW18 4JL
Postal only, or see me at Hugglets Festivals. Over 25 years experience.

CLEOPATRA BEARS

'The Paws', 35 Robertson Road, Perth, PH1 1SN
☎ 01738 638933
email: cleopatra.bears@tesco.net
Careful and sympathetic repairs for old and invalid bears.

CREATIONS PAST

The Dolls House, Stonehall Common, Worcestershire, WR5 3QQ
☎ **01905 820792**
email: mmbeardoll@aol.com
web: www.dollshousewallpaper.co.uk
Teddy bear clinic. Expert sympathetic restoration. Museum quality repairs to precious old Steiff, small Schuco, modern bears and dolls.

CYNNAMAN RESTORATION SERVICES

48A Underhill Road, South Benfleet, Essex, SS7 1EP
☎ 01268 754184
Bears all ages lovingly restored.

DAPHNE FRASER'S DOLL & BEAR HOSPITAL

'Glenbarry', 58 Victoria Road, Lenzie, Glasgow, Strathclyde, G66 5AP
☎ 0141 776 1281
Injured bears given loving care. Bears always happy in my hospital.

ANNA DICKERSON

Serenity, 17 Chapel Street, Barford, Norwich, Norfolk, NR9 4AB
☎ **01603 759647**
Loved bears repaired with care. Ailing bears received directly, by post or through 'The Bear Shop' at Norwich and Colchester.

DOLLY MIXTURES

3 Holly Road, Oldbury, West Midlands
☎ 0121 422 6959
Bears, dolls, bought, sold, restored. 26 years experience.

DOT BIRD

4 Cavendish Terrace, Ripon, North Yorkshire, HG4 1PP
☎ 01765 607131
email: dotsbears@btinternet.com
Specialising in sympathetic restoration of vintage teddy bears. As seen in 'Teddy Bear Scene'. Meet me at the Hugglets fairs.

● EVOLUTION BEARS RESTORATION SERVICE

☎ 0151 678 9452
email: evobear04@aol.com
web: www.evolutionbears.com
Quality restoration of old bears that reflects their age and condition. Visit our bear website, email, or phone for details.

● FARNBOROUGH BEARS

78 West Heath Road, Farnborough, Hampshire, GU14 8QX
☎ 01252 543454
email: farnboroughbears@ntlworld.com
or janettruin@ntlworld.com
Bear artist Janet offers loving restoration for all types of bears. Write or phone or email first. Reasonable rates.

● GERALDINE'S OF EDINBURGH

The Edinburgh Doll & Teddy Hospital
☎ 0131 333 1833
email: geraldine.e@virgin.net
web: www.dollsandteddies.com
Doll & teddy restorers.

● GRANNY'S GOODIES

Unit 3, 34a Camden Passage/Islington Green, London, N1 8DU
☎ 020 8693 5432 or 020 7704 2210 (shop)
Fax: 020 8693 5432
email: klaregerwat-clark@tinyworld.co.uk
web: www.grannysgoodiesfairs.com
Antique & artist bears. Brenda Gerwat-Clark. Open Wednesday and Saturday only. 8.30 - 4.00. Also teddy bear hospital.

● GUMDROP EDITIONS

The Cornwall Teddy Bear Hospital, Bygones, Fore Street, St Just, Penzance, Cornwall, TR19 7LJ
☎ 01736 787860
email: cornwallteddybearhospital-patients@yahoo.co.uk
web: www.just-arts.co.uk
Doctor Edwards of TBCI magazine, now at Cornwall Teddy Hospital. Expert sympathetic restorations. 25 years experience. Postal patients. Free estimates.

● IZZY'S CUBS

34 Sharphaw Avenue, Skipton, North Yorkshire, BD23 2QJ
☎ 01756 796548
email: mail@izzyscubs.com
web: www.izzyscubs.com
Satisfied customers world wide. Sympathetic repairs. No over working. All work guaranteed. Over thirty years experience. See my website.

● MARY SHORTLE OF YORK

9 Lord Mayors Walk, York, North Yorkshire, also at 5 Bootham, York and 9, 15 & 17 Queen's Arcade, Leeds.
☎ 01904 425168 / 631165 / 634045; Tel: 01132 456160 (Leeds) Fax: 01904 425168
email: mary@maryshortleofyork.com
web: www.maryshortleofyork.com
Expert teddy repairs. Over 20 years experience. Call for free estimates. Guaranteed satisfaction and personal service.

RESTORATION AND TEDDY BEAR ARTIST

Laura Boeck-Singers, 2326 N 58th St, Milwaukee, WI 53210, USA

☎ +1 414 871 4956 Fax: +1 414 445 8237
email: dsingers@ticon.net
web: www.teddy-bear-artists.com/LB-home.htm
Professional restoration of your cherished teddies, years of experience. Adult collectible creations, bears and pals, for the discriminating collector.

SAD PAD BEARS

☎ 01622 754441
web: www.sadpadbears.com
Specialists in vintage Teddy Bears and classic soft toys. Restoration and hand cleaning.

SEND 2 MEND BEARS

42 West Parade, Wisbech, Cambridgeshire, PE13 1QB
☎ 01945 475201 mobile 07906 290153
email: send2mendbears@aol.com
Repairs, renovations and cleaning of old bears and soft collectables. Fully insured. By mail or phone for appointment.

ST ANN'S DOLLS HOSPITAL

14 Hildreth Road, Prestwood, Gt Missenden, Bucks, HP16 0LU
☎ 01494 890220
email: alan.ann@dollshospital.freeserve.co.uk
web: www.dollshospital.freeserve.co.uk
Most repairs undertaken on old and modern bears and dolls. Please ring for an appointment. Monday - Friday only.

TERRY'S TEDDY HOSPITAL

16 Lower Green, Tewin, Welwyn, Hertfordshire, AL6 0LB
☎ 01438 718700 Fax: 01438 840411
email: tbrand@talk21.com
Sympathetic restoration by experienced restorer.

ELIZABETH THOMPSON

12 Briar Thicket, Woodstock, Oxford, Oxfordshire, OX20 1NT
☎ 01993 811915email: thompelix@aol.com
General care from geriatrics to new born: from 'wear and tear' to sudden accidents and attacks from dogs! Very reasonable rates.

WELLFIELD BEARS

'Wellfields', Unit 7, The Globe Centre, Wellfield Road, Cardiff, South Glamorgan, CF24 3PE
☎ 02920 453045
email: wellfield.bears@ntlworld.com
web: www.wellfieldbears.co.uk
Specialist conservation and restoration of teddy bears and dolls.

YESTERDAY'S CHILDREN

Mill House, Mill Lane, St. Ive's Cross, Sutton St. James, Nr Spalding, Lincolnshire, PE12 0EJ
☎ 01945 440466
All teddies, antique and modern dolls and soft toys restored with care. Please write or phone first.

END

Your business can appear in the next edition of the Guide

Contact Hugglets
to register your interest
and we will add you to our
business mailing list

Tel: +44 (0)1273 697974
Fax: +44 (0)1273 62 62 55
email: info@hugglets.co.uk

All Else That's Bruin

All Else That's Bruin incorporates a range of entries which are grouped as follows:

- Publications (mainly magazines and books)
- Illustrators and Portrait Artists (including greetings cards etc)
- Internet Services
- Museums (we recommend you check details directly before travelling a distance)
- Bear-related (including clothing, jewellery and other wares)
- Clubs

- PUBLICATIONS -

● HUGGLETS PUBLISHING
PO Box 290, Brighton, East Sussex, BN2 1DR
☎ **01273 697974 Fax: 01273 626255**
email: info@hugglets.co.uk
web: www.hugglets.co.uk
Publishers and Festival organisers. UK Teddy Bear Guide, Winter BearFest, Teddies 2008. Please join mailing list on our website for updates and announcements.

● PAT RUSH
36 Garrick Close, Towngate Wood Park, Shipbourne Road, Tonbridge, Kent, TN10 3RS
☎ 01732 361994/07715 704025
email: patrush@pavilion.co.uk
Writer specialising in teddy bears.

● TEDDY BEAR CLUB INTERNATIONAL
(incorporating Teddy Bear Times), Ashdown Publishing, Ancient Lights, 19 River Road, Arundel, West Sussex, BN18 9EY
☎ 01903 884988 Fax: 01903 885514
email: kirste@ashdown.co.uk
The UK's No. 1 bear magazine.

● TEDDY BEAR REVIEW
N7450 Aanstad Road, PO Box 5000, Iola, WI 54945-5000, USA
☎ +1 715 445 5000 Fax: +1 715 445 4053
email: shelleys@jonespublishing.com
web: www.teddybearreview.com
This magazine will show you how to find collectible bears, learn their cost, see new creations and learn how to make your very own teddies.

● TEDDY BEAR SCENE MAGAZINE
Warners Group Publications Plc, West Street, Bourne, Lincolnshire, PE10 9PH
☎ 01778 391158 Fax: 01778 392079
email: teddybearscene@warnersgroup.co.uk
web: www.teddybearscene.co.uk
The UK's favourite Teddy Bear publication for both new and established collectors. Packed with interesting and informative editorial features. Available on the news stand or via subscription.

● WEALDEN MANOR PRESS
2 Fircroft Close, Tilehurst, Reading, Berkshire, RG31 6LJ
☎ 0118 941 4000 Fax: As tel.
Unique hand crafted books. With real bears, teddies, story and myth. See us at Winter BearFest '08 or request brochure.

● AURORABEAREALIS
Kessock Post Office, Main Street, North Kessock, Inverness, Highland, IV1 3XN
☎ 01463 731470 Fax: As tel.
email: susan@aurorabearealis.co.uk
web: www.aurorabearealis.co.uk
Bear portraits in pastels from good photos or 'sitting'. Bear paintings and greetings cards. NEW handmade bears in cotton patchwork.

● BEAR PAWTRAITS
10 Chilham Avenue, Westgate-on-sea, Kent, CT8 8HD
☎ 0780 3780050
email: molly@bearpawtraits.com
web: www.bearpawtraits.com
Experienced fine artist, specialising in bear/doll pawtraits. Beautiful and large selection of cards/prints/originals available mail order. Commissions.

● BEAR-A-THOUGHT GREETINGS CARDS AND CALENDARS
PO Box 88, Newcastle-upon-Tyne, NE17 7WY
☎ 01207 563220
email: michael@bear-a-thought.co.uk
web: www.bear-a-thought.co.uk
Limited edition and unique greetings cards and calendars which are highly collectable, by the illustrator Michael Quinlyn-Nixon.

● CHESNEY DESIGNS
Greendales Hall, Mill Lane, Warton, Carnforth, Lancashire, LA5 9NW
☎ 01524 733152 Fax: As tel.
email: hmbears@btinternet.com
Humorous teddy cards and fridge magnets. Original designs by Ches Chesney (original jokes by Iris Chesney!).

● PRUE THEOBALDS
1 The Uplands, Maze Hill, St Leonards, East Sussex, TN38 0HL
☎ 01424 422306
Teddy Bear illustrator. Mail order books, prints, greetings cards. For commissions and licences contact Christopher Maxwell-Stewart at above address.

● BEARARTISTSOFBRITAIN.ORG
Bear Artists of Britain, 26 Wheatsheaf Court, Sunderland, Tyne & Wear, SR6 0RF
☎ 07725 640179
email: john@bearartistsofbritain.org
web: www.bearartistsofbritain.org
Independent showcase for British bears.

● DRAWING THE WEB, WEBSITE DESIGN
42 Palmarsh Avenue, Hythe, Kent, CT21 6NR
☎ 01303 269038 Fax: 01303 266669
email: barbaraannbears@msn.com
web: www.drawingtheweb.com
Do you need an exciting website to showcase your bears, or your own business stationery and greetings cards?

● HUGGLETS GUIDE - ONLINE EDITION
Hugglets, PO Box 290, Brighton, East Sussex, BN2 1DR
☎ 01273 697974 Fax: 01273 626255
email: info@hugglets.co.uk
web: www.hugglets.co.uk
At the Hugglets website you can launch the online edition to view, search and print pages from the Guide. Alternatively you can download a pdf file to your computer.

● THE BRITISH BEAR COLLECTION
Banwell Castle, Banwell, Somerset, BS29 6NX
☎ 01934 822263/822342
email: c_parsons@hotmail.co.uk
web: www.thebritishbearcollection.co.uk
The unique collection of British teddy bears and friends - currently on display at Wookey Hole Caves, nr Wells, Somerset.

"Is this the way to the Doll's House Museum?"

elcome

Welcome o Basel, Mr. Bearkin."

Puppenhausmuseum

Basel

- world's greatest collection of old **teddy bears**
- antique **toys**

dialog luckylook™

THE DORSET TEDDY BEAR MUSEUM
Eastgate, Corner of High East St & Salisbury St, Dorchester, Dorset, DT1 1JU
☎ 01305 266040 Fax: 01305 268885
email: info@teddybearmuseum.co.uk
web: www.teddybearmuseum.co.uk
See Edward Bear and his family of people-sized bears, with teddies from throughout the last century in this enchanting museum.

PUPPENHAUSMUSEUM
Steinenvorstadt 1, CH-4051 Basel, Switzerland
☎ +41 (0)61 225 95 95 Fax: +41 (0)61 225 95 96
web: www.puppenhausmuseum.ch
The collection, the only one of its kind in the world: teddy bears, doll's houses, shops, dolls and carrousels.

WOOKEY BEARS
Wookey Hole Caves, Wookey Hole, Wells, Somerset, BA5 1BB
☎ 01749 672243 web: www.wookey.co.uk
World famous bears to world famous caves and much more. Home to the British Bear Collection and many other bears.

ANN_KNITS 4 BEARS
14 Crete Lane, Dibden Purlieu, Southampton, Hampshire, SO45 4HW
☎ 02380 846987
email: ann@petri.fslife.co.uk
web: www.knits4bears.co.uk
Beautiful handknitted sweaters, cardies and pullovers especially for bears, my individual designs. Also crochet collars, hats, tailor-made garments. Enquiries welcome.

BEAR IT IN MIND
High Street, Beaulieu, Hampshire, SO42 7YA
☎ 01590 612097
email: info@bearitinmind.com
web: www.bearitinmind.com
'Bearly Scene' - exclusive jewellery collection by Silver Shadows Jewellery Design. Whimsical bear hidden in every piece. Please see shop listing.

CURTIS BRAE OF STRATFORD
32 Sheep Street, Stratford upon Avon, Warwickshire, CV37 6EE
☎ 01789 267277
email: sales@curtisbrae.co.uk
web: www.curtisbrae.co.uk
Collectable and traditional gollies and Russian dolls. Soft sculpture animals by Hansa Toys and Steiff. Beatrix Potter characters.

TRAFFORD PRINT & DESIGN
69 John Gray Road, Great Doddington, Wellingborough, Northamptonshire, NN29 7TX
☎ 01933 229366 Fax: As tel.
email: info@traffordprint.co.uk
web: www.traffordprint.co.uk
Business cards, swing tags, leather tags, ribbon labels, shirt printing etc. Brochure and samples £2.50 or download free from website.

TREVOR JENNER DESIGNER JEWELLERY
PO Box 764, Crawley, West Sussex, RH10 0WL
☎ 01342 713858
email: tj@trevorjennerdesignerjewellery.com
web: www.trevorjennerdesignerjewellery.com
Please see display advertisement.

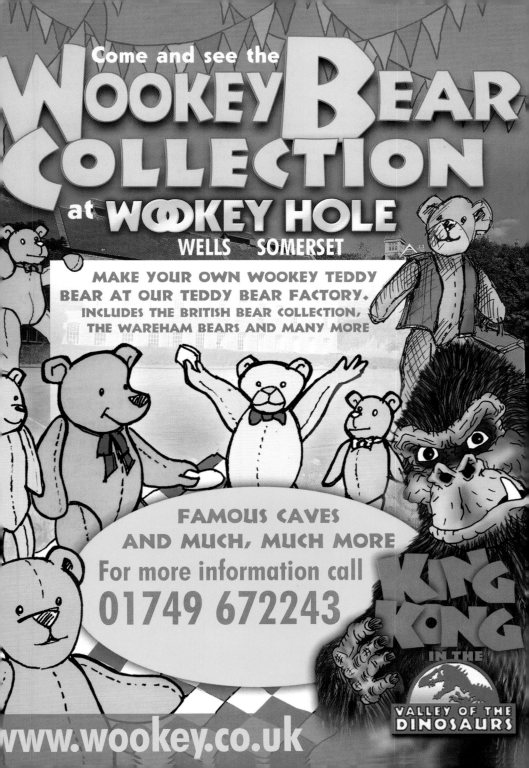

● ABC
email: artist_bears@yahoo.co.uk
web: www.geocities.com/artist_bears
Miniature Bear Club. Selection of members handcrafted artist bears, bunnies, gollies and friends. More details on website or please e-mail.

● THE BEAR CLUB
email: fred@thebearclub.co.uk
web: www.thebearclub.co.uk
A club for anyone that has a teddy or an interest in wild bear conservation. What's your teddy done today?

● BRITISH TOYMAKERS GUILD
PO Box 240, Uckfield, TN22 9AS
☎ 01225 442440
email: info@toymakersguild.co.uk
web: www.toymakersguild.co.uk
SAE for membership information.

● DEAN'S COLLECTORS CLUB
PO Box 217, Hereford, HR1 9AB
☎ 01981 240966 Fax: 01981 241076
email: teddies@deansbears.com
web: www.deansbears.com
Membership includes a free mohair bear and badge, competitions and colour magazine. Great Britain's Biggest teddy bear club.

● GOOD BEARS OF THE WORLD (UK) TRUST
Brian Beacock, 76 Shortwood Avenue, Staines, Middlesex, TW18 4JL
☎ 01934 822342 (Carolyn Parsons)
email: alison-bob@amarsay.freeserve.co.uk
Charitable organisation distributing bears to comfort those in need. Annual membership £10, overseas £12. Three newsletters issued yearly.

● JUST GOLLY COLLECTORS CLUB
60 Arundel Road, Littlehampton, West Sussex, BN17 7DF
☎ 01903 721070   email: justgolly@hotmail.com
Quarterly 24 page newsletter. News, views and information. Competitions with prizes. Covers all areas of golly collecting. SAE for details.

● PERM TEDDY BEAR CLUB
email: teddyclub@mail.ru
web: www.teddyclub.narod.ru
We are in Russia. Established 2004. Hares, cats... and chiefly Teddy Bears!!!

● ROBIN RIVE COLLECTORS CLUB
Countrylife New Zealand Ltd, 2nd floor, 145-157 St John Street, London, EC1V 4PY
☎ 0121 288 0548
email: briguk@robinrive.com
web: www.robinrive.com
Membership includes annual bear, catalogues, newsy Oakdale Farm Chronicle, exclusive member-only offers. Year runs from July. Join online.

● STEIFF CLUB UK
Astra House, The Common, Cranleigh, Surrey, GU6 8RZ
☎ 01483 266643 Fax: 01483 266650
email: leyla.maniera@steiff.com
web: www.steiff-club.de
Please see back cover advertisement.

THE TEDDY BEAR ORPHANAGE

92 Heath Street, Nutgrove, St Helens, Merseyside, WA9 5NJ
☎ 01744 812274 Fax: 01744 813334
email: info@teddybearorphanage.co.uk
web: www.teddybearorphanage.co.uk
Parents of Teddies Association. Membership £44.50 for free bear, termly newsletters, special offers, discount vouchers, Christmas and postcards.

THE WORLD SOCIETY FOR THE PROTECTION OF ANIMALS

WSPA Albert Embankment, London, SE1 7TP
☎ 0800 316 9772 Fax: 020 7793 0208
email: fundraising@wspa.org.uk
web: www.wspa.org.uk/fundraising
Teddy Bears Picnics, Name That Bear, Teddy Bear Auctions. Help real life bears for charity, please get in touch.

END

Hugglets PUBLISHING

Bear Gallery

Welcome to our Gallery showcasing the wide variety of teddy bear styles available.

Please see the Bear Makers and Artists section for contact details (starting page 105).

AM Bears

All Bear by Paula

A Hitchcock Bear

Barnwell Bears

Barbara Ann Bears

PUBLISHING Hugglets

Bear Bits

Bärenhäusl - Ositos-Bären

Barling Bears

Bears by Susan Jane

Barrel Bears

Bearly Sane Bears

Bears of Bath

Bears N' Company

Beatrix Bears

Bears of Eastwood

Bebbin Bears

Beautifully Bear

Bears of the Abbey

Bell Bears

Beddingfield Bears

Bedford Bears

Bedspring Bears

Bessy Bears

Bunky Bears

Bradgate Bears

BigFeetBears

Bisson Bears

Bumble Bears

Bolebridge Bears

Brewers Bruins

CC Bears Australia

Burlington Bearties

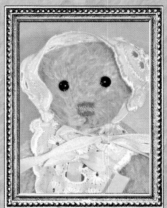

Candi Bears

Burlington Bears

Canterbury Bears

Dari Laut Bears

Charlie Bears

Cripple Creek Creative

Do Do Bears

E.J. Bears

Doodlebears & Friends

PUBLISHING Hugglets

Dusty Attic Bears

Eildon Bears

Granny Grumps Bears

Futch Bears

Elliebears

Flutter-By Bears

HM Bears

Guardian Angel Bears

Gyll's Bears

Haven Bears

F.J. Hannay Bears

Hairy Hugs

Hansa Toys

Happy Tymes® Collectibles

Hoovigs

Hoblins

Hazelwood Bears

Hermann Teddy Original

J.C.W. Bears

Hugs Unlimited

Huntersfield Bears

Jac-2-Lyn Bears

Jan's Tiddy Bears

Pam Howells

Jenny Loves Benny

Ju-beary Bears

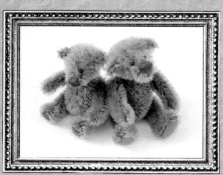

Isabelle Bears

Kerrow Bears

Jenni Bears

Kaysbears

Kingston Bears

Knutty Bears

Karin Kronsteiner Bears

Lora Bears

Madabouit Bears

Lyndee-Lou-Bears

Pennbeary

Mary Myrtle Miniatures

Mister Bear

Pertinax Bears

PC Bangles

Namtloc Bears

Pick-me Bears

~Pipedream Bears

Pipkins Bears

Petal Originals

Pywacket Bears

Sue Quinn

Hugglets PUBLISHING

The Rabbit Maker

Robin Rive Bears

Annette Rauch

Rowan Bears

Sarah's Bears of Cambridge

Saint Bear

Tillington Bears

Scruffie Bears by Susan Pryce

Teds of the Riverbank

Scruffy Bears

Thing About Bears

Three O'Clock Bears

Hugglets PUBLISHING

Shantock Bears

Teeny Bears

Julie Shepherd

Scrumpy Bears

Shebob Bears

Toggle Teddies

Veryibears

Top 'n' Tail Teddies

Toys, Stuffed ... by Susan

Westie Bears

Heartfelt Bliss by Trendle

Whittle-Le-Woods Bears

END

Hugglets PUBLISHING

Bear Makers & Artists

Also including golllies, animals and other creations. International entries are indicated by a globe.

● A BETTER CLASS OF BEAR
Hillside, Hatch Lane, Chapel Row, Bucklebury, Berkshire, RG7 6NX
☎ 01189 713182
email: pam@hillier-brook.freeserve.co.uk
Limited edition quality collectors bears.

● A HITCHCOCK BEAR
2 Church Hill Road, Oxford, OX4 3SE
email: ahitchcockbear@yahoo.co.uk
web: www.ahitchcockbear.com
Bears that smile to make you smile. Cute, cuddly, homemade OOAK bears ready for adoption. Personalised and commissioned mohair bears.

● ABELIA BEARS
21 Rochford Close, Broxbourne, Hertfordshire, EN10 6DL
☎ 01992 478229
email: gallop@talk21.com
Beautiful bears for all occasions. Traditional and modern bears.

● ACTUALLY BEARS BY JACKIE™
Hunnypot House, 18 Lowry Way, Stowmarket, Suffolk, IP14 1UF
☎ 01449 675951
web: www.actuallybearsbyjackie.co.uk
Handsewn miniature and full-size bears and home to the famous Tubby Teds!™

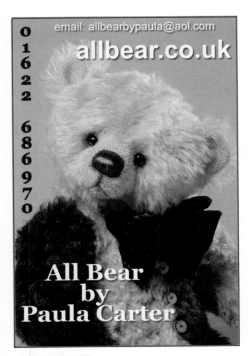

email: allbearbypaula@aol.com
allbear.co.uk
01622 686970
All Bear by Paula Carter

A Hitchcock Bear
www.ahitchcockbear.com
2 church hill rd, oxford, ox4 3se, uk

ALEXANDER BEARS

197 Avenue Road, Erith, Kent, DA8 3DA
☎ 01322 337797
email: alexbearuk@aol.com
web: www.freewebs.com/alexanderbears
Beautiful mohair bears and needle-felted miniature bears. Loveable, huggable bears, handcrafted by Eileen Alexander. Please visit my website.

ALL BEAR BY PAULA CARTER

21 Hazelwood Drive, Allington, Maidstone, Kent, ME16 0EA
☎ 01622 686970 Fax: As tel.
email: allbearbypaula@aol.com
web: www.allbear.co.uk
Putting the Teddy back into Bear! Designer bears for the adult collector. Please visit the All Bear website!

ALL THINGS BEARY

33 Pentland View, Edinburgh, Lothian, EH10 6PY, Scotland
☎ 0131 477 6970
email: hugs@allbeary.com
web: www.allbeary.com
Bears for all, many miniatures, themed bears, T-shirts, china, cards, much more. Original handcrafted designs. Website updated. Mail order.

ALWAYS BEARING IN MIND

Margaret Ann Coltman, 68 Cressex Road, High Wycombe, Buckinghamshire, HP12 4TY
☎ 01494 437238
email: teddies@alwaysbearinginmind.co.uk
web: www.alwaysbearinginmind.co.uk
Happy hugs and beary bits. Mainly hand-stitched character and celebration bears plus other 'beary bits' as 'inspired'!

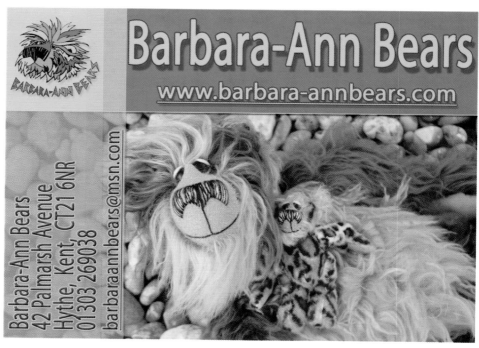

Barbara-Ann Bears
www.barbara-annbears.com

Barbara-Ann Bears
42 Palmarsh Avenue
Hythe, Kent, CT21 6NR
01303 269038
barbaraannbears@msn.com

AM BEARS

18 Spa Croft, Tibshelf, Alfreton, Derbyshire, DE55 5NZ
☎ 07837 194433
email: am_bears@yahoo.com
web: www.ambears.co.uk
One-off handcrafted bears, bunnies and friends in quality fabrics, made for you to love. Commissions undertaken. Created by Andrea Lewis.

AMANDA'S HONEY POT BEARS

Amanda Ferguson, Ruach, 5 Springfields, Liscolman, County Antrim, BT53 8EX
☎ 028 207 42927
email: honeypotbears@tiscali.co.uk
web: www.honeypotbears.com
Pssst The Honey Pot Bears are in their cottage waiting to take you on a trip of childhood memories.

ANGIEBEARS

27 Trubridge Road, Hoo St Werburgh, Rochester, Kent, ME3 9EN
☎ 01634 253165
email: angie@angiebears.net
web: www.angiebears.net
Bear artist making quality bears.

ANN MADE BEARS

60 Layfield Road, Hendon, London, NW4 3UG
☎ 020 8202 3165
email: ann@ann-made-bears.co.uk
web: www.ann-made-bears.co.uk
Original handcrafted artist bears designed and made by Ann Reed available at bear fairs and by mail order. Commissions taken.

ANN'S RIDGEHILL BEARS

3 South Stour Cottage, Mersham, Ashford, Kent, TN25 7HU
☎ 01233 721900
Traditionally hand made mohair bears. One of a kind, made to order. Ideal for birthdays, christenings, weddings etc.

Bearly Sane Bears
by Sharon Aish

Loveable Traditional & Character Bears

Tel: 01752 403515

Exclusive limited editions and commissions available by request

www.bearlysanebears.com

Bears N' Company

Ingrid Norgaard Schmid, Ontario, Canada

Tel: +1-705-726-1499   ischmid@hotmail.com

Hugglets PUBLISHING

ANNA KOETSE'S BEARS

Anna Koetse, Willem de Zwijgerlaan 8, 2012 SC, Haarlem, Netherlands

☎ +31 (0)23 5472048 Fax: +31 (0)23 5472034

email: koetse@xs4all.nl

web: www.annakoetse.com

Special, funny, inspiring, mostly dressed originals for collectors and museums. 100% handmade by artist. Many sizes. Visit gallery at website.

AROUND THE GARDEN BEARS

93 Cornwall Avenue, Peacehaven, East Sussex, BN10 8SE

☎ 01273 585259

Mohair bears made with love. Various sizes some dressed. Assorted bear clothing, bear gifts. Orders taken.

ATLANTIC BEARS

5 Braeside, Gairloch, Ross-shire, IV21 2BG, Scotland

☎ 01445 712179

email: info@atlanticbears.co.uk

web: www.atlanticbears.co.uk

Callers welcome by appointment.

AURORABEAREALIS

Kessock Post Office, Main Street, North Kessock, Inverness, Highland, IV1 3XN

☎ 01463 731470 Fax: As tel.

email: susan@aurorabearealis.co.uk

web: www.aurorabearealis.co.uk

Bear portraits in pastels from good photos or 'sitting'. Bear paintings and greetings cards. NEW handmade bears in cotton patchwork.

BAGGALEY BEARS

6 Boundary Road, Beeston, Nottingham, Nottinghamshire, NG9 2RF

☎ 0115 8757 031

email: v.fletcher-baggaley@talk21.com

web: www.freewebs.com/baggaleybears

Quality hand-crafted miniature bears.

BAILEY BEARS

3 Turnberry Drive, Bricket Wood, St Albans, Hertfordshire, AL2 3UT

☎ 01923 673437 Fax: As tel.

email: claire@romantiquebrides.co.uk

Mohair jointed teddy bears made to order and bear repairs.

BALU BEARS

Thomas Balke & Susanne Ludwig, Theisenstrasse 9, D-38108 Braunschweig, Germany

☎ +49 (0) 531 34 26 90

web: www.balu-baer.de

Beautiful traditional bears aged with care, inspired from antique bears. Please visit our website for new collection.

BARBARA-ANN BEARS

42 Palmarsh Avenue, Hythe, Kent, CT21 6NR

☎ 01303 269038 Fax: 01303 266669

email: barbaraannbears@msn.com

web: www.barbara-annbears.com

Wild but gorgeous bears. Hand dyed mohair, kits, one to one bear making classes and website design.

Bears of Eastwood

Tel: 01482 847535
http://web.mac.com/bearsofeastwood
email: bearsofeastwood@mac.com

BÄRENHÄUSL-OSITOS®-BÄREN
Pfarrer-Braun-Str. 12, 83043 Bad Aibling, Germany
☎ +49 (0)80 61 34 33 10 Fax: +49 (0)80 61 34 33 11
email: ositos-teddys@web.de
web: www.ositos-baeren.de
Meet us at Hugglets Teddies Festival or ask for a shop near you!

● BARLING BEARS
by Marilyn Lambert, 13 Pear Tree Avenue, Ditton, Aylesford, Kent, ME20 6EB
☎ 01732 845059 Fax: As tel.
email: marilyn@barlingbears.co.uk
web: www.barlingbears.co.uk
Finest quality mohair collectors' bears, individually designed and created by Marilyn. Each bear a unique personality for you to treasure!

● BARNWELL BEARS
Trenance, 57 Mill Lane, Upton, Chester, Cheshire, CH2 1BS ☎ 01244 380422
email: donandmel@fsmail.net
Award winning collectors bears from 3" - 20" individually designed and handmade by Melanie Smith. Please see Gallery picture. All enquiries welcome.

● BARREL BEARS
69 Long Innage, Halesowen, West Midlands, B63 2UY
☎ 01384 410438
email: danni-home@fsmail.net
web: www.barrelbears.co.uk
Special handmade mohair / faux fur one-of-a-kind bears with needlefelted faces, some with swivel ears. All cuddle tested.

● BARRON BEARS
2296 Eastbrook Road, Vista, CA 92081, USA
☎ +1 760 598 9123
email: barronbears@cox.net
web: www.barronteddybears.com
Handmade and designed by artist Sharon Barron. Traditional bears, bear purses, old looking bears and much more.

● BAYBEE BEARS
25 Fuller Mead, Harlow, Essex, CM17 9AR
☎ 07729 117410
email: abracadabra@ntlworld.com
web: www.baybeebears.piczo.com
Quality OOAK bears & friends handmade with love. Commissions welcome. Reference: Hugglets for free web postage. Ebay I.D. Madshoerepairer.

● BEAR BAHOOCHIE
40 Glamis Gardens, Polmont, Falkirk, FK2 0YJ, Scotland
☎ 01324 411823
email: kateri@bearbahoochie.co.uk
web: www.bearbahoochie.co.uk
Unique personalised miniature bears made on a commission basis. Miniature rats and other critters available on request. Usual price £35.

● BEAR BITS
The Florins, Silver Street, Minting, Horncastle, Lincolnshire, LN9 5RP
☎ 01507 578360 Fax: As tel.
email: ashburner@bearbits.freeserve.co.uk
web: www.bearbits.com
Wonderful bears. See display advertisement.

● BEAR CRAZEE

Wakefield, West Yorkshire
☎ 0798 607 2712 (mob)
email: bears@bearcrazee.com
web: www.bearcrazee.com
*Award winning artist bears individually creat-
ed with love and attention for the discerning
collector, no two bears alike. Commissions
welcome.*

● BEAR IN MIND

360 London Road, Deal, Kent, CT14 9PS
☎ 01304 366234
email: bearinmind@btinternet.com
*One-offs and special commission bears for
the discerning collector. Handmade in the
traditional way but full of modern character.*

● BEAR TREASURES BY MELANIE JAYNE

☎ 01942 862354
email: melanie@beartreasures.com
web: www.beartreasures.com
Bears with charm and personality.

● BEARABLE BEARS

Burg. Jhr. Quarles van Uffordlaan 31, 7321 ZS.
Apeldoorn, Netherlands
☎ +31 (0)55 5788067
email: bearablebears@hotmail.com
web: www.bearablebears.nl
*I hope my self designed bears can give you
a little journey to the past.*

● BEARITZ

Iona, Whitelea Road, Burrelton, By Blairgowrie,
PH13 9NY
☎ 01828 670561
email: janice@bearitz.com
web: www.bearitz.com
*Handcrafted bears designed and created
with finest mohairs. Zany to soulful characters by Janice Davidson. Secure online shopping. Enquiries welcome.*

● BEARLY SANE BEARS

107 Plymstock Road, Oreston, Plymouth, Devon,
PL9 7PQ
☎ 01752 403515
email: bearlysanebears@googlemail.com
web: www.bearlysanebears.com
Collectors bears by Sharon Aish.

BÄRENHÄUSL

Ositos®-Bären
handmade & designed by Angela Schulz
www.ositos-baeren.de   ositos-teddys@web.de
Phone +49 (0)8061-343310
Fax +49 (0)8061-343311

BEARLY THERE

5 Park Road, Netherton, Dudley, West Midlands, DY2 9BY

☎ 01384 236532 Fax: As tel.

email: lorraine@bearlythere.com

web: www.bearlythere.com

Miniature bears 1" to 5". Handsewn in upholstery fabric and mohair by Lorraine Jones. One off and limited editions.

BEARS ABUNDANT

Ruth Fraser, 156 Shaughnessy Blvd, North York, Ontario, M2J 1J8, Canada

☎ +1 416 493 2944

Original old look bear designs, fully jointed 12" scale dollhouse bears, loving restoration, identification and evaluation of old bear friends.

BEARS BY EUNICE

219 Salmon Street, London, NW9 8ND

☎ 020 8205 6308 Fax: As tel.

email: eunice.edwards308@btinternet.com

Handcrafted character bears and others. Limited editions. Best quality mohair, fun furs. Made with loving care.

BEARS BY HAND

41 Thetford Close, Danesholme, Corby, Northamptonshire, NN18 9PH

☎ 01536 461159

Traditional and collectors bears in mohair and other fine fabrics. Limited editions and special commissions. Large SAE for photographs, etc.

BEARS BY JULIA

3 Suffolk Avenue, West Mersea, Colchester, Essex, CO5 8ER

☎ 01206 386654

Individually hand stitched collectors bears.

BEARS BY JULIE-ANN

9 Hollybank Grove, Halesowen, West Midlands, B63 1BT

☎ 0121 602 0443 mob: 07949 427173

email: jhat1@hotmail.co.uk

Hand made mohair or alpaca bears with needle felted faces and paws. All bears are OOAK.

BEARS BY SUSAN JANE KNOCK

6 Elizabeth Avenue, Witham, Essex, CM8 1JE

☎ 01376 521230

email: susan.k@tinyworld.co.uk

Unique little character bears 1"-7", also exquisite miniature range of 1" animals and toys. Please ring, email, sae for details.

BEARS N' COMPANY

Ingrid Norgaard Schmid, 59 Melinda Crt., Barrie, Ontario, L4N 5T7, Canada

☎ +1 705 726 1499

email: ischmid@hotmail.com

'Days gone by' inspire Ingrid Norgaard Schmid to use vintage fabric and accessories to create enchanting heirloom teddies.

BEARS OF BATH

☎ 01761 417271

email: carol@bearsofbath.co.uk

web: www.bearsofbath.co.uk

Handmade original bears inspired by the City of Bath. Created by artists Carol and Paul Birkeland-Green.

BEARS OF EASTWOOD

2 The Forge, Old Village Road, Little Weighton, Hull, East Riding, HU20 3UJ
☎ 01482 847535
email: bearsofeastwood@mac.com
web: http://web.mac.com/bearsofeastwood
Made with love, for you to love! Please feel free to contact me! Commissions taken. World wide shipping. Paypal accepted.

BEARS OF THE ABBEY

by Canadian Artist Susan Mckay, 160 Frederick Street, Suite 501, Toronto, Ontario, M5A 4H9, Canada
☎ **+1 416 703 1697 Fax: +1 416 703 8228**
email: mckayabbey@rogers.com
web: www.bearsoftheabbey.com
Award winning characters: bears, miniature dogs, cats, dolls, rabbits and more. All handcrafted original designs. Commissions and wholesale inquiries welcomed.

BEARS PAW COLLECTABLES

The Retreat, 60 Naseby Road, Leicester, Leicestershire, LE4 9FH
☎ 0116 274 1441 Fax: As tel.
email: keith.w.freeman@btinternet.com
Maker of fine quality collector's bears in small limited editions using only the finest quality mohair. Since 1992.

BEARS UNLIMITED

14 Clausen Way, Pennington, Lymington, Hants, SO41 8BJ
☎ 01590 670536
email: bearsunlimited@sky.com
Handmade mohair collectors bears. Stitched with love. Lead or steel weighted. Individually hand-dyed and small limited editions. Selected fairs attended.

BEARS UPON SOAR

5 Hickling Drive, Sileby, Loughborough, Leicestershire, LE12 7PA
☎ 01509 670481/07866 616799
email: lisa@bearsuponsoar.co.uk
web: www.bearsuponsoar.co.uk
Realistic bears made from the highest quality mohair and alpaca, handcrafted with meticulous attention to detail by artist Lisa Wills.

BEAUTIFULLY BEAR

Alynfa, Wrexham Rd, Abermorddu, Wrexham, Flintshire, LL12 9DF

One of a kind bears

Kitties, Ratties, Pandas and Friends

Tel: 07765 381951
www.beautifully-bear.co.uk
beautifully_bear@yahoo.co.uk

Bebbin Bears
By Yvonne Andrew
www.bebbinbears.co.uk

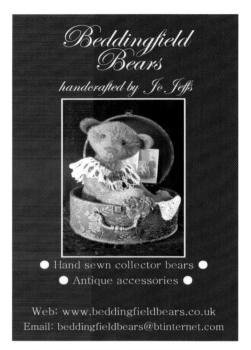

Beddingfield Bears

handcrafted by Jo Jeffs

● Hand sewn collector bears ●
● Antique accessories ●

Web: www.beddingfieldbears.co.uk
Email: beddingfieldbears@btinternet.com

● BEARS WITH ATTITUDE

24 Ferncroft Walk, Chellaston, Derby, Derbyshire, DE73 6SA
☎ 01332 690624 Fax: As tel.
email: suehargar@aol.com
Collectable bears, kits and supplies.

● BEATRIX BEARS

283 Monkmoor Road, Shrewsbury, Shropshire, SY2 5TF
☎ 01743 340276
email: beatrix.bears@virgin.net
web: www.beatrixbears.co.uk
Traditional and character artist bears. Worldwide delivery. All major credit cards accepted. Trade enquiries welcomed.

● BEAUT BEARS

Lange Haven 72ab, 3111 CH Schiedam, Netherlands
☎ +31 (0)610 623 559
email: marianne@beautbears.nl
web: www.beautbears.nl
Artist designed collectors bears. Handmade one-offs of finest mohair and alpaca, some with needlefelted and trapunto features. View pictures on www.beautbears.nl

● BEAUTIFULLY BEAR

Alynfa, Wrexham Road, Abermorddu, Flintshire, Wrexham, LL12 9DF
☎ 07765 381951
email: beautifully_bear@yahoo.co.uk
web: www.beautifully-bear.co.uk
Designed and created by Elizabeth Adams of A.B.C. Bears. Kitties, Ratties, Pandas, Bears and friends, one-of-a-kind in top quality mohairs.

● BEBBIN BEARS

by Yvonne Andrew, 7 Middle Road, Aylesbury, Buckinghamshire, HP21 7AD
☎ 01296 423755
email: bebbinbearsuk@aol.com
web: www.bebbinbears.co.uk
Exquisite, unique, award winning artist bears, designed and created for collectors. Each having their own special character, personality, and charm!

● BEDDINGFIELD BEARS

80 Beaumont Walk, Leicester, LE4 0PQ
☎ 0796 3723220
email: beddingfieldbears@btinternet.com
web: www.beddingfieldbears.co.uk
Traditional hand sewn collector bears with antique accessories. Each bear is unique. A beautiful addition to any hug! Commissions welcome.

● BEDFORD BEARS

Church Farm, Eyeworth, Sandy, Bedfordshire, SG19 2HH
☎ 01767 318626 Mob: 07972 452297
email: ann@bedfordbears.co.uk
web: www.bedfordbears.co.uk
Traditional bear makers since 1985. Patterns and designs made exclusively from original drawings by the bear artist Ann-Marie Owen.

● BEDRAGGLE BEARS™

36 North Road, St Andrews, Bristol, BS6 5AF
☎ 0117 9497389
email: suehoskins@hoskinsuk.co.uk
Old souls stitched with love into unique little bears with big hearts and a story to tell of past times.

BEDSPRING BEARS

Carretera a la Escalona 39, El Roque, San Miguel De Abona, Tenerife 38620, Canary Isles
☎ +34 922 701 004
email: bedspringbears@btopenworld.com
web: www.bedspringbears.com
Handcrafted artist bears, cats, gollies etc.

BEDSTEAD BEARS

email: bearinfo@bedsteadbears.com
web: www.bedsteadbears.com
Traditional mohair bears hand crafted by Charlotte Dakin in Oxfordshire. Sold exclusively via the web - www.bedsteadbears.com

BEES KNEES BEARS

7 Madeira Avenue, Codsall, Wolverhampton, West Midlands, WV8 2DS
☎ 01902 843124 Fax: As tel.
email: bkbears@btinternet.com
web: www.beesknees bears.co.uk
Original designs by Jo Matthews.

BELL BEARS

The Workshop, 55 Tannsfeld Road, Sydenham, London, SE26 5DL
☎ 020 8778 0217 Fax: 020 8659 2278
email: bellbears@btinternet.com
Traditional handcrafted artist bears by Doreen Swift. Commissions and enquiries welcome. Send ten 1st class stamps for details and photographs.

BELLY BUTTON BEARS

Fox Hollow, Greenfields, Earith, Huntingdon, Cambridgeshire, PE28 3QZ
☎ 01487 842538
email: patkipps@tiscali.co.uk
Exclusive hand crafted finest mohair bears. Unique one-offs and small limited editions. Created by Pat Kipps. Big Hug!

BENJAMIN BEARS

61 Diana Road, Chatham, Kent, ME4 5PW
☎ 01634 832523
email: benjaminbears@btinternet.com
web: www.benjaminbears.bravehost.com
Unique adorable bears, see website.

BERRY LANE BEARS

12 Avondale Road, Vange, Basildon, Essex, SS16 4TT
☎ 01268 558007
email: ju006b1390@blueyonder.co.uk
web: www.berrylanebears.co.uk
Unique designs, bears, gollies and friends. Hand made with loving care by Angela D. Underdown.

BESSY BEARS

Little Strickland Hall, Little Strickland, Penrith, Cumbria, CA10 3EG
☎ 07900 815445
Handmade mohair artist bears. Editions of one to five. Filled with cotton, steel shot, attitude and courage. Commissions welcome.

BETTY'S BEARS

12 Long Acre Road, Carmarthen, SA31 1HL
☎ 01267 221721
email: betty.mcniven@talk21.com
Luxurious, individually hand-crafted bears, unique and affordable.

BIG TREE BEARS

101 Howbeck Road, Arnold, Nottingham, Nottinghamshire, NG5 8QA
☎ 0115 952 4022
email: cm.holbrook@ntlworld.com
Christine Holbrook's beautiful collectors bears, hand crafted in the finest quality mohairs and alpacas. One-offs and small limited editions.

BIGFEETBEARS

Dedham Art & Craft Centre, High Street, Dedham, Essex, CO7 6AD
☎ 07855 209293
email: ruth@kilby-rawcliffe.demon.co.uk
web: www.bigfeetbears.com
OOAK hand-sewn teddy bears made in mohair. Specialising in realistic bears. Commissions welcome.

BILBO BEARS

3 Outwood Avenue, Clifton, Greater Manchester, M27 6NP
☎ 0161 794 7931
Quality mohair bears designed and lovingly made by Audrey Edwards for national and international collectors.

BILLY BUFF BEARS

Calle Barcelona, 91, 17130 L'Escala, Girona, Spain
☎ +34 972 770923
web: www.billybuffbears.com
Quality handcrafted traditional fully jointed bears by Hazel Slough.

BISSON BEARS

347C Hjellestadvegen, Hjellestad, 5259 Bergen, Norway
☎ +47 47967755 UK mobile: 07788 501435
email: bissonbears@hotmail.com
web: www.bissonbears.com
Please see display advertisement.

BOBBYS BEARS

4 Station Road, Blackrod, Bolton, Lancashire, BL6 5BN
☎ 01204 468090 Fax: 01204 695744
email: bobbys.bears@virgin.net
web: www.bobbysbears.co.uk
Hand crafted traditional teddy bears.

BOLEBRIDGE BEARS

48 Rosemary Road, Amington, Tamworth, Staffs, B77 3HF
☎ 01827 59097
email: vina.hollis@ukonline.co.uk
Individually designed affordable mohair bears.

BONSALL BEARS

21 Cliffefield Road, Meersbrook, Sheffield, S8 9DJ
☎ 0114 2508532
email: susan@bonsallbears.com
web: www.bonsallbears.com
Extra Terrestrial Teddies have landed at http://bonsallbears.smugmug.com and more down to earth ones too!

BOX BEARS

Top Floor, 208 Fernhead Road, London, W9 3EJ
☎ 07956 555230 Fax: 0208 962 0797
email: sharon@boxbears.co.uk
web: www.boxbears.co.uk
Bears, hares & friends. Handcrafted original designs using the finest materials. Member British Toymakers Guild. Visit new website.

BRADGATE BEARS

'The Lily Pot', 20 Ruskin Field, Anstey, Leicester, LE7 7QP
☎ 0116 236 7147
email: judy@bradgatebears.co.uk
web: www.bradgatebears.co.uk
Nostalgic little bears and bigger friends.

BRADLEY BEARS

11 St Marys Close, Weston, Spalding, Lincs, PE12 6JL
☎ 01406 373073
email: michele.partridge@tiscali.co.uk
web: www.bradleybears.co.uk
Award Winning Bears - mostly one offs made from finest mohair and alpaca. Please come and visit my bears on www.bradleybears.co.uk

BRAVEHEART BEARS

3 The Oaks, Thorndon, Nr Eye, Suffolk, IP23 7JR
email: cheryl@braveheartbears.co.uk
web: www.braveheartbears.co.uk
Individual handmade traditional teds!

Collectors Bears handmade by Doreen Swift

BellBears
The Workshop, 55 Tannsfeld Road, Sydenham, London SE26 5DL, England
Telephone: 020 8778 0217 email: bellbears@btinternet.com
Send ten 1st class stamps for details & photographs

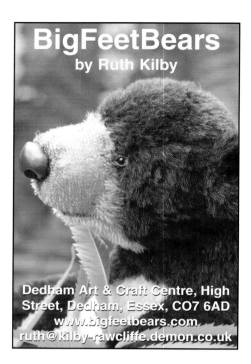

BREWER'S BRUINS
by Andrea Brewer, 155 Bolens Creek Road, Burnsville,
NC 28714, USA
☎ +1 704 433 6507
email: bearsbyandrea@aol.com
web: www.BrewersBruins.com
*Small bears of character. Enquiries most
welcome. Credit cards accepted. Worldwide
shipping.*

BRIDGWATER BEARS
100 Bridgwater Road, Ipswich, Suffolk, IP2 9QF
☎ **01473 412066**
email: lm.dye@ntlworld.com
***Lots of new bears and old favourites all in
super mohair including many one offs.***

BRIERLEY BEARS
86 Barnsley Road, Brierley, Barnsley, South Yorkshire,
S72 9JY
☎ 07841 159666
email: brierleybears@hotmail.co.uk
web: www.freewebs.com/brierleybears
*High quality artist bears designed and hand
crafted by Kat Vardy. All bears come with
personalised birth certificate. Commissions
undertaken.*

BROOKLYN BEARS
Combe Acre, Whiston, Northampton, NN7 1NN
☎ 01604 891585
email: lilymay6@aol.com
Handmade bears cute cuddly lovable.

BROTHERWOOD BEARS
47 Poynder Place, Hilmarton, Calne, Wiltshire,
SN11 8SQ
☎ 01249 760284 Fax: 01249 760530
email: suebrotherwood@aol.com
web: www.brotherwoodbears.com
*Original lovable bears - fairy bears, baby
bears. Please take a look at my website!*

BROW BEARS
9 Ireleth Brow, Askam in Furness, Cumbria, LA16 7HB
☎ 01229 467861
email: juliejames1978@yahoo.co.uk
Traditional mohair teddy bears.

BROWNE BEARS & FRIENDS

Crossrigg House, Westnewton, Wigton, Cumbria, CA7 3LA
☎ 016973 20484
email: brownebears@tiscali.co.uk
web: www.brownebears.org.uk
Artist bears and gollies by Jenifer Browne. Limited editions, one-offs, shop exclusives, patterns and kits. Trade enquiries welcome.

BRUINS ALL ROOND

5 Melrose Gardens, Roker, Sunderland, SR6 9LD
email: pipkin@whiskers.eclipse.co.uk
web: www.whiskers.eclipse.co.uk
Collectable bears and rabbits. Small limited editions and OOAK. Sold in aid of animal rescue. See website for more information.

BUCKIE BEARS

18 Reidhaven Street, Ianstown, Buckie, Morayshire, AB56 1SB, Scotland
☎ 01542 835639 Fax: As tel.
email: niki@buckiebears.co.uk
web: www.buckiebears.co.uk
Mohair artist bears by Niki Sadler. Send sae for new leaflet.

BUMBLE BEARS

17 Adur Close, West End, Southampton, Hampshire, SO18 3NH
☎ 02380 326663
email: fiona@bumblebears.co.uk
web: www.bumblebears.co.uk
Traditional collectors bears by Fiona Wells, designed and handmade with great care and attention to detail, since 1995. See advertisement.

BUNKY BEARS

104B Northgate, Newark, Nottinghamshire, NG24 1HF
☎ 01636 678724
email: enquiries@bunkybears.co.uk
web: www.BunkyBears.co.uk
Traditional and contemporary artist bears.

BrewersBruins.com

by Andrea Brewer

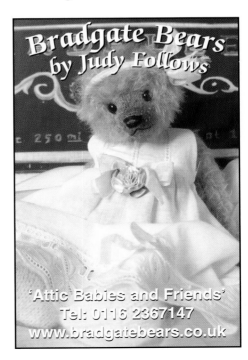

BURLINGTON BEARTIES

2 Ambergate Drive, Kingswinford, West Midlands, DY6 7HZ

☎ 01384 279731

email: bridgemark@bearties.freeserve.co.uk

Antique style realistic characters for collectors. Bears, cats and rabbits all individually dressed in vintage clothing.

BURLINGTONBEARS.COM

25 Kipling Drive, Wimbledon, London, SW19 1TJ

☎ 0870 0671873

email: tania@burlingtonbears.com

web: www.burlingtonbears.com

Exclusively designed wild and wacky bears and other creatures lovingly hand-crafted in the finest quality materials. Commissions welcomed.

BURRA BEARS

Hamnavoe, Burra Isle, Shetland, ZE2 9JY

☎ 01595 859374

email: info@burrabears.co.uk

web: www.burrabears.co.uk

Delightful, collectable bears handmade in the Shetland Island of Burra and produced from recycled traditional Fair Isle knitwear.

BUTTON BEARS

Ericastraat 68, 6581 BX Malden, Netherlands

☎ +31 (0)612 439297

email: button_bears@yahoo.com

web: www.buttonbears.nl

Handmade artist design miniature bears & friends. Also special design bear crafts kits.

CALA BEAR DEN

18 Bibeau Bay, Winnipeg, Manitoba, R2J 2A7, Canada

☎ +1 204 257 6003

email: calabear@mts.net

web: www.calabear.ca

OOAK bears to inspire that OOAK smile. Bears in sizes 5" to 12" made from best quality mohair.

When contacting advertisers please mention you saw their advertisement in the UK Teddy Bear Guide

CANDI BEARS

Steffi McIntyre, 43 Brewlands Crescent, Symington, Kilmarnock, South Ayrshire, KA1 5RN
☎ 01563 830729 or 07769 574274
email: steffi@candibears.co.uk
web: www.candibears.co.uk
Hand crafted collectors bears. Traditional and character styles. All bears one of a kind. See web site for more details.

CANTERBURY BEARS

The Workshop, Builders Square, Littlebourne, Nr Canterbury, Kent, CT3 1XU
☎ **01227 728630**
email: **enquiries@canterburybears.com**
web: **www.canterburybears.com**
Canterbury Bears 100% made in England. They always have been and always will be.

CARAMAC BEARS

Firwood Cottage, Firwood, First Drift, Wothorpe, Stamford, Lincolnshire, PE9 3JL
☎ 01780 767183/750758 Fax: 01780 767183
email: caramacbears@tiscali.co.uk
web: www.freewebs.com/caramacbears
Original one off hand dyed, hand stitched collector's bears. In gorgeous colours and wonderful, different styles. Well worth looking at.

CARMICHAEL BEARS

54 Limekiln Row, Castlefields, Runcorn, Cheshire, WA7 2LT
☎ 01928 563874
email: karen@carmichaelbears.co.uk
web: www.carmichaelbears.co.uk
Handcrafted mohair teddy bears.

CC BEARS AUSTRALIA

P.O. Box 202, Bright, Victoria 3741, Australia
☎ +61 3 5759 2574
email: cindybears@dodo.com.au
web: www.ccbearsaustralia.com
Unique original artistic dawgs, kitty's and tra-ditional bears, with adorable faces. Made with quality mohair & alpaca by Cindy Cherry.

CHAPPLE BEARS

Belvedere, 43 Trelissick Road, Hayle, Cornwall, TR27 4HY
☎ **01736 755577**
Bears of distinction wearing hallmarked silver collars. Individually designed. Unique and beautifully made by the artist Beryl Chapple. Details £2.

CHARLIE BEARS LIMITED

Unit 5 Circuit Business Park, Clawton, Holsworthy, Devon, EX22 6RR
☎ 01409 271420
email: sales@charliebears.com
web: www.charliebears.com
Affordable artist designed collectors bears in mohair and plush. Bespoke designs and one off projects also undertaken.

CHATHAM VILLAGE BEARS L.L.C.

Artist Art Rogers, 2722 Chatham Dr., Maryland Heights, MO 63043-1208, USA
☎ +1 314 739 8426 Fax: +1 314 291 1580
email: geoart1@swbell.net
web: www.chathamvillagebears.com
These animals would be a great addition to any collector's collection.

CHELTENHAM BEARS

7 Edendale Road, Golden Valley Park, Cheltenham, Gloucestershire, GL51 0TX
☎ 07905 307859
email: suerowe@ip3.co.uk
web: www.cheltenhambears.co.uk
Beautiful mohair bears, hand stitched to highest quality by Sue. Visit my online shop. Commissions taken.

CHERRY'S CHUMS

Avda Virgen de Antigua 20, Altavista 10, Caleta de Fuste, Antigua 35610, Fuerteventura, Canary Islands, Spain
☎ +34 928163269 mob: +34 6379 67093/07885 710630
email: cherryswinn@hotmail.com
Mohair bears and cats lovingly made by Cherry Swinnerton.

CHESTER BEARS

40 Meadows View, Marford, Wrexham, Clwyd, LL12 8LS
☎ 01978 855604
email: chesterbears@moviebus.com
Traditional hand made bears using top qual-ity materials. Small limited editions.

CHRISTINE PIKE BEARS

Puddlefoot, Bridge Road, Downham Market, Norfolk, PE38 0AE

☎ 01366 380229 Fax: As tel.

email: christine@christinepike.com

web: www.christinepike.com

Character and traditional artist bears. Award winning artist bears. Also freelance journalism and illustration: bears and dolls my speciality.

CLEMENS BEARS OF GERMANY

c/o A M International Agencies Ltd., Digital House, Peak Business Park, Foxwood Rd, Chesterfield, Derbyshire, S41 9RF

☎ 01246 269723 Fax: 01246 269724

email: enquiries@am-international-agencies.com

web: www.clemens-spieltiere.de

World famous traditional and artist bears from Germany's leading company, Clemens. Finest quality mohair and the most appealing bears guaranteed!

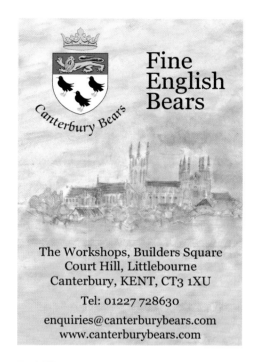

● CLEOPATRA BEARS

'The Paws', 35 Robertson Road, Perth, PH1 1SN
☎ 01738 638933
email: cleopatra.bears@tesco.net
Hand crafted and hand dyed limited edition mohair teddy bears and their other furry friends.

● COLYNS COTTAGE BEARS

Colyns Cottage, 12 Kinnear Street, Buckhaven, Fife, KY8 1BH
☎ 01592 566621
email: L7kee@msn.com
web: www.colynscottagebears.co.uk
Miniature needle felted lovingly handcrafted bears. One of a kind designs by bear artist Lynn Smith. Commissions welcomed.

● CONRADI CREATIONS

21 Telford Avenue, Streatham Hill, London, SW2 4XL
☎ 020 8671 2794
email: karin_conradi@hotmail.com
web: www.conradicreations.com
Beautiful quality handstitched traditional bears with handpainted faces. Commissions undertaken.

● CORNELIA BEARS - HOLLAND

Dedemsvaartweg 314, NL-2545 AJ, Den Haag, Netherlands
☎ +31 (0)70 32 95 857 Fax: As tel.
email: info@corneliabears.com
web: www.corneliabears.com
Miniature bears. Own design. Materials: mohair, upholstery and suede. Also crocheted bears. Accept PayPal, Visa and Mastercard. Handmade with love.

● COUNTRY BEARS

6 Meadow Croft, Weston-super-Mare, Somerset, BS24 9XE
☎ 01934 811785
email: supertedds@dsl.pipex.com
web: www.freewebs.com/country-bears
Primitive, whimsical and vintage style creations by Clare Davis-Tedd.

● COVENTRY BEARS

2 Warriston Avenue, Edinburgh, EH3 5ND
☎ 07947 066675
email: lauracoventry@yahoo.co.uk
Laura's miniature bears and animals, sent worldwide. My own mainly one-off, hand-stitched designs. Commissions welcome. Please call/email for details.

● COWSLIP BEAR COMPANY/CHRISTINE HAWKES

2 Warren Avenue, Mudeford, Christchurch, Dorset, BH23 3JX
☎ 01202 382073 or 07776 108528
email: cowslipbears@ntlworld.com
web: www.cowslipbears.co.uk
Hand made mohair or alpaca bears 6" to 31" all one of a kind - Cowslip Bears - the original Smiley Bears!

Cripple Creek Creative
feltings by Mikki
"they make you smile"

email - RTwodie@aol.com
cripplecreekcreative.com

Dari Laut Bears

E.V.A. Dressed Bear Winner 2002
Readers Choice Dressed Bear Winner 2003

Traditional and character bears
and animals. Dressed
and undressed.

Designed
and lovingly
created
by Patricia
Banks

Tel:
01424
754418

www.dari-laut-bears.co.uk
Email: pat@dari-laut-bears.co.uk

CRIPPLE CREEK CREATIVE
Mikki Klug, 1641 St.Rt.133, Bethel, Ohio 45106, USA
email: rtwodie@aol.com
web: www.cripplecreekcreative.com
Softly Sculpted Felties that make you smile. Feature unique poses and personalities. Would love to create your favorite Fuzzy ...Mikki.

CROTCHETY BEARS
4 Spring Grove Crescent, Kidderminster,
Worcestershire, DY11 7JB
☎ 01562 752289
Hand made collectors teddy bears.

DAISA ORIGINAL DESIGNS LTD
Appletree Lodge, Westfield Lakes, Barton-upon-Humber, North Lincolnshire, DN18 5RG
☎ 01652 661881 Fax: 01652 661882
email: sales@itsadodl.com
web: www.theoriginalreikibear.com and
www.itsadodl.com
The original Reikibear™ and It's a dodl © bear are exclusive bears and available only from Daisa Original Designs.

DARI LAUT BEARS
Dari Laut, 25 De Chardin Drive, Hastings, East Sussex, TN34 2UD
☎ 01424 754418
email: pat@dari-laut-bears.co.uk
web: www.dari-laut-bears.co.uk
Traditional and character bears and animals designed and lovingly created by award winning artist Patricia Banks. Enquiries welcome. Photographs available.

DASHING DUCK
Rue du Languedoc, 34210 Siran, France
☎ +33 (0)4 68 49 15 67
email: info@dashingduck.com
web: www.dashingduck.com
Traditional artist designed collectors bears. Bespoke orders taken. Worldwide shipping. Please see our website for further information.

DEAN'S RAG BOOK CO (1903) LTD

PO Box 217, Hereford, HR1 9AB
☎ 01981 240966 Fax: 01981 241076
email: teddies@deansbears.com
web: www.deansbears.com
Great Britain's Oldest teddy bear company.

DI NIC'S BEARS

PO Box 1923, Coff's Harbour, NSW 2450, Australia
☎ +61 (0)2 665 12463 Fax: +61 (0)2 665 12898
email: karen@dinicsbears.com
web: www.dinicsbears.com
Hand made original designer bears filled with personality and love.

DO DO BEARS

27 Linden Close, Colchester, Essex, CO4 3LZ
☎ 01206 524261
email: dodo.bears@ntlworld.com
web: www.dodobears.com
Happy bears that are full of character for you to enjoy. Retail and Trade enquiries welcome. Visit our website today!

DOODLEBEARS & FRIENDS

21 Churchill Avenue, Aylesbury, Buckinghamshire, HP21 8NF
☎ 01296 397082
email: doodlebears_uk@hotmail.com
web: www.doodlebears.co.uk
Collectable bears by Jane-Lynne Martin.

DREAMTIME

Sue Woodhouse, 12 Yeoman Road, Northolt, Middlesex, UB5 5TJ
☎ 020 8842 2327 (Bear)
email: dreamtime@dsl.pipex.com
web: www.dreamtime.dsl.pipex.com
Handcrafted bears, dragons and furry friends. Collectors miniatures and micro's 1"- 6" fully jointed. One-offs and special very small limited editions.

DRURY BEARS

85 Pembury Road, Tonbridge, Kent, TN9 2JF
☎ 01732 364042 Fax: As tel.
email: sarah@drurybears.co.uk
web: www.drurybears.co.uk
Quality limited edition collectors bears. Wedding and bespoke bears made of your choice.

VÉRONIQUE DUBOSC

103 rue Abbé de l'épée, 33000 Bordeaux, France
☎ +33 (0)5 56 51 04 65
email: v_dubosc@yahoo.fr
web: www.foliesdours.com
Traditional collectors' bears in the finest mohairs. Dressed with a romantic French touch. One-offs.

DURRERBEARS AND MORE

South Perth, WA, Australia
☎ +61 (0)8 9368 1557 Fax: As tel.
email: durrerbears@iinet.net.au
web: www.durrerbears.com
Artist bears and gollies, all original designs and hand crafted by award winning artist. Patterns, kits and workshops available.

DUSTY ATTIC BEARS

Rosemary Cottage, Oxenpill, Meare, Glastonbury, Somerset, BA6 9TQ
☎ 01458 860532
email: chloe@chloewilson.wanadoo.co.uk
web: www.dustyatticbears.co.uk
One of a kind bears.

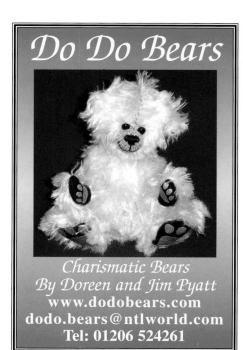

● E. J. BEARS
8 Marsh Close, Waltham Cross, Hertfordshire, EN8 7JF
☎ 01992 714354
Traditional hand made bears.

● ECOBEARS
Aptdo. Correos 18, 43750-01 Flix, Tarragona, Spain
☎ +34 617 836 923 or +34 977 057 044
email: ecobears@hotmail.com
web: www.ecobears.com
Earth friendly collectors' bears; beautiful artwork; an illustrated environmental story from planet Vynen; and interesting gifts handmade using solar energy.

● EDEN BEARS
337 Marine Road, Central Promenade, Morecambe, Lancashire, LA4 5AB
☎ 01524 418377 Mob: 07761 211696
email: edenbears@onetel.com
Traditionally-styled, fully jointed collector bears in mohair and plush lovingly made by Elaine. Request a PDF brochure by email.

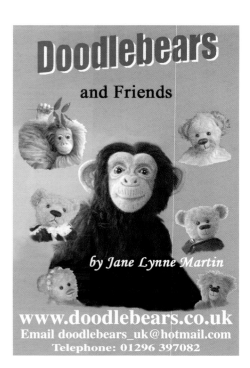

● EILDON BEARS
69 Eildon Crescent, Melrose, TD6 9RG
☎ 01896 823832
email: eildonbears@tiscali.co.uk
Unique and limited edition traditional bears handmade from mohair, tweed or linen. Cute and cuddly in plush. Commissions welcome.

● ELIZBET BEARS
128 Elm Drive, Risca, Newport, Gwent, NP11 6PA
☎ 01633 615208
email: aileen.terry@talk21.com
web: www.elizbet-bears.co.uk
Collector bears all one off.

● ELLIE-BEARS
272 Southend Road, Wickford, Essex, SS11 8PS
☎ 01268 762438
email: ellie@elliebears.com
web: www.elliebears.com
Loveable collectors mohair and alpaca artist bears and Furry Friends carefully created. Commissions welcome.

● ENCHANTED PLACE BEARS
Demelia Cottage, Florence Place, Falmouth, Cornwall, TR11 3NJ
☎ 01326 210462
email: bears@enchantedplace.co.uk
web: www.enchantedplace.co.uk
At Enchanted Place Bears we create individ-ually designed, entirely hand-made collec-tors' bears of the finest quality.

● ESKOLE NOOMBAS
11 Jalan Pergam, 488370, Singapore
☎ +65 6545 5904 Fax: +65 6542 2918
email: alicia@eskolenoombas.com
web: www.eskolenoombas.com
Playful and beautifully realistic bears plus other animals. Airbrushed, unique and very life-like. Please visit my website!

● ESSENTIAL BEARS
Wendy & Megan Chamberlain, 20 Belmont Road, Mowbray, 7700 Cape Town, South Africa
☎ +27 (0)21 685 3487 Fax: As tel.
email: ebears@iafrica.com
web: www.essentialbears.net
Award winning miniature bears and other animals. Patterns and kits available.

FAIR BEARS

17 Athorpe Grove, Dinnington, Sheffield, South Yorkshire, S25 2LD
☎ 01909 564472
Quality bears for discerning collectors.

FAIRYLAND BEARS

Unit 3, The Sloop Craft Market, St Ives, Cornwall, TR26 2TF
☎ 07720 957072 / 01736 799901
email: hayley@fairylandbears.fsnet.co.uk
web: www.fairylandbears.co.uk
All of our one of a kind bespoke creations are truly original and a must have for discerning collectors.

FARNBOROUGH BEARS

78 West Heath Road, Farnborough, Hampshire, GU14 8QX
☎ 01252 543454
email: janettruin@ntlworld.com
or farnboroughbears@ntlworld.com
Exclusive collectors mohair bears handmade and designed by Janet Truin. Small limited editions and one offs. Contact Janet as above.

FENBEARY FOLK

2 Fortyfoot Cottages, Pointon Fen, Sleaford, Lincolnshire, NG34 0LF
☎ 0845 157 6871
email: pemblington@thefens.wanadoo.co.uk
web: www.fenbearyfolk.co.uk
One of a kind beary folk in mohair, alpaca and luxury faux fur. 6"- 15". Collector's bears - traditional and modern styles.

FINE AND DANDY BEARS

5 Manor Road, Burton Coggles, Grantham, Lincs, NG33 4JR
☎ 01476 550079
email: jan@finedandybears.com
web: www.finedandybears.com
Delightful mohair bears. Finely made to a high standard, wearing traditional dandy vintage silk cravats. Please see website for details.

E.J. Bears

By Eileen Jackman
Tel: 01992 714354

Elliebears

Lovable Handmade
Collectable
Mohair Bears
Commissions
welcome

www.elliebears.com
Tel: 01268 762438 email: ellie@elliebears.com

Flutter-By Bears

Delightful miniature bears and friends.
www.flutter-by-bears.co.uk
Tel: 01782 560 136
email: ruthbowman@tiscali.co.uk

FUTCH BEARS

by Di Futcher
difutcher@dsl.pipex.com
www.futchbears.co.uk
Tel: 01277 219032

● FLUTTER-BY BEARS

by Ruth Bowman, 26 Ludford Close, Newcastle-under-Lyme, Staffordshire, ST5 7SD
☎ 01782 560136
email: ruthbowman@tiscali.co.uk
web: www.flutter-by-bears.co.uk
Original miniature collectors' bears and friends 1 to 3 inches sewn with loving attention to detail. Have a tiny hug!

● FOREST GLEN BEARS

1 Ditchbury, Lymington, Hampshire, SO41 9FJ
☎ 07967 972611
email: jo@forestglenbears.co.uk
web: www.forestglenbears.co.uk
Adorably cute limited edition and one-off bears made in the heart of the New Forest. Special orders and commissions welcome.

● FRED-I-BEAR/FREDI'S WORKBASKET

Lynette Kennedy, PO Box 6502, Westgate, 1734, South Africa
☎ +27 (0)83 2500378 Fax: +27 (0) 11 672 4008
email: lck@mweb.co.za
web: www.fred-i-bear.co.za
Limited edition handmade artist bears & your one stop bear supply shop.

● FUTCH BEARS

32 Hillside Walk, Brentwood, Essex, CM14 4RB
☎ 01277 219032
email: difutcher@dsl.pipex.com
web: www.futchbears.co.uk
Artist bears with antique accessories.

● G-RUMPY BEARS

4 Puller Road, Barnet, Herts, EN5 4HF
☎ 020 8275 0693 Fax: As tel.
email: jane@g-rumpy.demon.co.uk
web: www.g-rumpy.co.uk
Bears that bring a smile.

● GARRINGTON BEARS

16 Garrington Close, Vinters Park, Maidstone, Kent, ME14 5RP
☎ 01622 685194
Quality collector bears, mostly one of a kind, made with care for a lifetime of loving.

GEMSTONE BEARS
Stepping Stones, 73 Pydar Close, Newquay, Cornwall, TR7 3BT
☎ 01637 877743
email: lesley@gemstonebears.fsnet.co.uk
web: www.gemstonebears.com
Unique limited collector's bears hand sewn with a real gemstone heart to add uplifting character to any hug. Commissions welcome.

GERALDINE'S OF EDINBURGH
☎ 0131 333 1833
email: geraldine.e@virgin.net
web: www.dollsandteddies.com
Creators of the 'Young at Heart' limited edition collection. New additions always available. Please send for details. Trade enquiries welcome.

GILL'S GOLLIES
101 Wainwright, Werrington, Peterborough, Cambridgeshire, PE4 5AH
☎ 01733 702490
email: gillsgollies@ntlworld.com
Special miniature gollies with unique smiles for you and your bears. Also the home of The Cheeky Golly Goblins!

GLENDAVENY TEDDY BEARS
41 Broad Street, Peterhead, Aberdeenshire, AB42 1JB
☎ 01779 481608 Fax: 01779 838406
email: info@glendaveny.co.uk
web: www.glendaveny.co.uk
Glendaveny Bears are traditionally crafted bears using finest quality mohair with board and pin jointing in a variety of sizes.

GOLLY GALORE
PO Box 174, Hailsham, East Sussex, BN27 9AE
☎ 01227 760186
email: info@gollygalore.com
web: www.gollygalore.com
www.teddygalore.com starting shortly. Franchisees wanted for United Kingdom, Ireland and Europe. Hand made bears/gollies. Top quality artists.

● GRACE DAISY BEARS

Lorraine Morris, 51 Gilbert Close, Basingstoke, Hampshire, RG24 9PA
☎ 01256 476140
web: www.lorrainemorris.com
Traditional, individually made mohair bears.

● GRANNY GRUMPS BEARS

31 Stobart Close, Beccles, Suffolk, NR34 9LT
☎ 01502 715347
email: shonawinter@ukonline.co.uk
Original designs by Award Winning Artist Shona Winter. Dressed and undressed mohair collectables. L/E and OOAKs. See Bear Gallery.

● GREENLEAF BEARS

17 High Mount Street, Hednesford, Staffs, WS12 4BH
☎ 01543 877343
email: pjwarrington@email.com
web: www.greenleafbears.co.uk
Traditional bears with a twist.

● JO GREENO

2 Woodhill Court, Woodhill, Send, Surrey, GU23 7JR
☎ 01483 224312
email: jo.greeno@btinternet.com
International artist and designer specialising in one of a kind dressed bears, animals and gollies. Established 1990.

● GREGORY BEAR

5 Primrose Road, Walton-on-Thames, Surrey, KT12 5JD
☎ 01932 243263
email: gregory@hugoshouse.com
web: www.hugoshouse.com
Classic and character teddy bears designed and made by Gregory Gyllenship.

● GUARDIAN ANGEL BEARS

14 Bank Street, St Columb, Cornwall, TR9 6AU
☎ 01637 881114
email: guardianangelbears@hotmail.co.uk
web: www.guardianangelbears.com
Beautiful hand made mohair Guardian Angel Bears with fabulous hand crafted feather wings by bear artist Susie Bedford-Stradling.

● GUND (UK) LIMITED

Gund House, Units 3-4 Carnfield Place, Walton Summit Centre, Bamber Bridge, Preston, Lancashire, PR5 8AQ
☎ 01772 629292 Fax: 01772 627878
email: sales@gunduk.com
web: www.gund.com
Collector bears, premium soft toys.

● GYLL'S BEARS

74 Kenilworth Crescent, Enfield, Middlesex, EN1 3RG
☎ 0208 366 1836 Fax: 0208 364 6234
Handmade mohair bears.

● H M BEARS

Greendales Hall, Mill Lane, Warton, Carnforth, Lancashire, LA5 9NW
☎ 01524 733152 Fax: As tel.
email: hmbears@btinternet.com
Original bears by Iris Chesney. Please see display advertisement and see us at the very best teddy bear fairs.

● HAIRY HUGS

35 Fullerton Close, Southampton, Hampshire, SO19 9JP
☎ 07765 434441
email: hairyhugs@aol.com
web: www.hairyhugs.co.uk
Hand made bears by Amanda.

● HAMPTON BEARS

15 Bownham Mead, Rodborough Common, Stroud, Gloucestershire, GL5 5DZ
☎ 01453 872615
email: ginnie.ebbrell@dsl.pipex.com
Bears, gollies and critters for the discerning collector. Commissions accepted. Made with love.

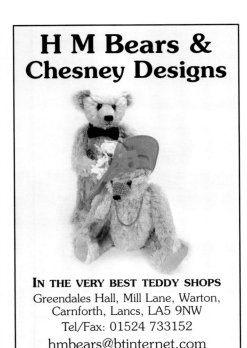

● F.J. HANNAY BEARS

31 William Street, Redcar, North Yorkshire, TS10 3BS
☎ 01642 480622
email: enquiries@fjhannaybears.com
web: www.fjhannaybears.com
Handcrafted artist bears with character.

● HANSA TOYS

UK distributors: Action Agents Ltd, Brian & Antony Somers, 16 Station Parade, Whitchurch Lane, Edgware, Middlesex, HA8 6RW
☎ 020 8954 5956 Fax: 020 8954 4606
email: info@hansa-uk.com
web: www.hansa-uk.com
Incredibly realistic, beautifully crafted, wonderfully detailed plush animals: Hand-trimmed fur; 'Toys that Teach' tags; Lifesize & 'rideable' animals. Made in Philippines.

● HAPPY TYMES®
COLLECTIBLES

by Beverly White , 399 Echo Dell, Downingtown, PA 19335, USA
☎ +1 610 873 0407
email: bev@happytymes.net
web: www.happytymes.net and www.teddiestogo.net
Original Art Teddy Bears & Portrait Bears® since 1984, plus Teddies To Go®

● HARDY BEARS

by June Kendall, 6 Clausen Way, Lymington, Hampshire, SO41 8BJ
☎ 01590 670615
Exclusive collectors mohair bears handmade and designed by June Kendall. One off's and small limited editions. Trade enquiries welcome.

● HAVEN BEARS

Newhaven, Hough Lane, Norley, Frodsham, Cheshire, WA6 8JZ
☎ 01928 788313 Fax: As tel.
email: info@havenbears.com
web: www.havenbears.com
Handmade mohair bears from the heart of Cheshire. Allour bears are 'one of a kind', made with love.

● HAZELWOOD BEARS

11 Hazelwood Close, Crawley Down, West Sussex, RH10 4HF
☎ 01342 712413
email: christine@hazelwoodbears.com
Exquisite bears by Christine Jenner.

● HERMANN TEDDY ORIGINAL

Teddy-Hermann GmbH, Postfach 1207, D-96112 Hirschaid, Germany
☎ +49 (0)9543 84820 Fax: +49 (0)9543 848210
email: info@teddy-hermann.de
web: www.teddy-hermann.de
Traditional mohair bears in limited editions, miniatures, accessories etc. UK Main Agent: Brian Somers. Tel: 020 8954 5956. Please see advertisement on page 137.

● HERMANN TEDDY ORIGINAL

UK Main Agent Brian Somers, 1 Georgian Close, Stanmore, Middlesex, HA7 3QT
☎ 0208 954 5956
email: briansomers@actionagentsltd.freeserve.co.uk
web: www.teddy-hermann.de
Please see advertisement on page 137.

● HILDEGARD GUNZEL BEARS

c/o A M International Agencies Ltd., Digital House, Peak Business Park, Foxwood Rd, Chesterfield, Derbyshire, S41 9RF
☎ 01246 269723 Fax: 01246 269724
email: enquiries@am-international-agencies.com
web: www.hildegardguenzel.com
Hildegard Gunzel's unique style is now popular with collectors and first time buyers. Her amazing designs are sure to attract!

● HILLTOP TOYS

Manor Cottage, Benn Lane, Farley, Wiltshire, SP5 1AF
☎ 01722 712265 Fax: As tel.
High quality mohair bears and other soft toys plus bear furniture.

● HOBLINS

5 Byron Avenue, Warton, Preston, Lancashire, PR4 1YR
☎ 01772 635516
email: bears@hoblins.freeserve.co.uk
Lovely outfits or just bare, weighty mohair bears from four to twenty inches. All handmade in Lancashire by Linda Willetts.

UK Distributors : Action Agents Limited, Brian and Antony Somers
16 Station Parade, Whitchurch Lane, Edgware, Middx HA8 6RW
Tel:020 8954 5956   Fax:020 8954 4606   Email:info@hansa-uk.com

www.hansa-uk.com

"Portraits in Nature"

ansa Toy's world renowned
ollection of incredibly realistic,
eautifully crafted, eminently
uddly plush animals.

nimals from every corner of the globe.

rom 4 inches to 4 metre display items.

oys that Teach" tags on every item.

any life size / "rideable" animals
hildren or adults up to 250lbs).

/onderfully detailed faces.

and-trimmed fur.

ased in the Philippines, Hansa is strongly opposed to child labour and sub-standard work practices and believes
nat the treatment of its workers is reflected in the products they produce. This has led to the formation of a
ighly motivated loyal force of experienced artisans, all of whom think of themselves as part of the Hansa family.

● HOLDINGHAM BEARS
Unit 6, Navigation Yard, Carre Street, Sleaford, Lincolnshire, NG34 7TR
☎ 01529 303266
email: barbara@holdinghambears.com
web: www.holdinghambears.com
Limited edition and one of a kind quality mohair bears lovingly hand produced by Barbara Daughtrey. Commissions accepted. Enquiries welcome.

● HOLLY BEARS
Rosebank Cottage, 70 Heath Road, Uttoxeter, Staffordshire, ST14 7LT
☎ 01889 568848
Handmade one-off bears, cats, rabbits.

● HONEY POT BEARS
106 Purbrook Way, Havant, Hampshire, PO9 3SB
☎ 02392 472455/07881 644164
Beautiful handmade mohair collectors' bears by Melanie C. Willis. Lifelike or traditional. Limited editions/made to orders. Sae please for brochure.

F. J. Hannay Bears
EST.1995

www.fjhannaybears.com
*31, William Street
Redcar
North Yorkshire
TS10 3BS*
Tel:01642 480622
Private & trade orders welcome

● HOVVIGS
Yvonne Graubaek, Hovvigvej 68, 4500 Nykoebing Sj, Denmark
☎ +45 5991 3494 or in UK: 07785 788307
email: hovvigs@post.tele.dk
My UK Agent: Round About Bears, Suffolk. Please ask for free colour list, or see www.roundaboutbears.co.uk

● HUG-A-BOO BEARS
68 Hitchen, Merriott, Somerset, TA16 5RA
☎ 01460 72740
Handcrafted and adorable collectors bears.

● HUGGLETS
PO Box 290, Brighton, East Sussex, BN2 1DR
☎ **01273 697974 Fax: 01273 626255**
email: **info@hugglets.co.uk**
web: **www.hugglets.co.uk**
Thousands of artist bears available at the Winter BearFest and Teddies 2008. Organised by Hugglets, the publishers of the UK Teddy Bear Guide. Please join mailing list on our website for updates and announcements.

● HUGGY BEARS
117 Diamond Avenue, Kirkby-in-Ashfield, Nottinghamshire, NG17 7LX
☎ 07796 952427 Fax: 01623 458514
email: bonniray@yahoo.co.uk
Distinctive old style dressed mohair bears. Jointed dressed gollies. Small repairs undertaken. Ring or email for details.

● HUGS UNLIMITED
Dawn James, 13 Bacup Road, Todmorden, West Yorkshire, OL14 7PN
☎ 01706 839938
email: dawn@hugsunlimited.co.uk
web: www.hugsunlimited.co.uk
Original Traditional Mohair Artist Bears dressed or undressed, by Award Winning Bear Artist, Dawn James, commissions undertaken, trade enquiries welcome.

14663 6
Kaspar, 52cm
Limited Edition:
500 pcs.

design: Traudel Mischner-Hermann

HERMANN *Teddy* ORIGINAL®

The Teddy-Hermann Collectors' Club is in its 8ᵗʰ year and is still growing. Wouldn't you also like to become a member? Come and join our Teddy-Hermann family – we would be pleased to welcome you.

An exclusive gift awaits you: a high-quality **"HERMANN Teddy ORIGINAL"** Bear of 13 cm size. You have the right to acquire an Exclusive Club Edition which is only available to members of the Teddy-Hermann Collectors' Club and receive twice a year our newsletter called "Barenpost" as well as our latest catalogues and updates.

For further information please contact your shop and ask for an application form to join the Club

Club Gift 2007
13 cm

Teddy-Hermann GmbH
Postfach 1207, D-96112 Hirschaid, Germany

UK Main Agent: Brian Somers, 1 Georgian Close, Stanmore, Middx, HA7 3QT
Tel: 0208 954 5956 email: briansomers@actionagentsltd.freeserve.co.uk

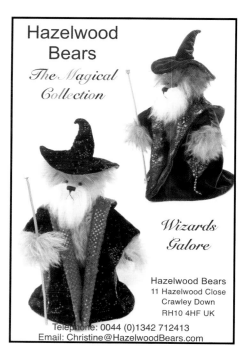

HUMBLE-CRUMBLE COLLECTORS BEARS

by Victoria Allum, 78 Chalkwell Avenue, Westcliff-on-Sea, Essex, SS0 8NN
☎ 01702 715383
email: vkallum@hotmail.com
web: www.victoriaallum.co.uk
Award winning traditional mohair bears.

HUNTERSFIELD BEARS

57 Huntersfield, South Tehidy, Camborne, Cornwall, TR14 0HW
☎ 01209 711557
email: cfdell@clara.net
web: www.huntersfieldbears.com
Unique handcrafted bears with character.

HYEFOLK

1 Ainsdale Close, Folkestone, Kent, CT19 5LU
☎ 01303 277925
Bears that make you smile!

INGE BEARS

PO Box 817, Kleinmond 7195, South Africa
☎ +27 (0)721 104273
email: ingebears@hermanus.co.za
web: www.ingebears.homestead.com
One-of-a-kind miniature bears, designed by Ingrid Els.

ISABELLE BEARS

15 The Grassmarket, Edinburgh, EH1 2HS
email: thebearshop@gmail.com
web: www.enchantedwood.net
Traditional jointed, individually handcrafted teddy bears. Workshops and classes available regularly and on request.

IZZY'S CUBS

34 Sharphaw Avenue, Skipton, North Yorkshire, BD23 2QJ
☎ 01756 796548
email: mail@izzyscubs.com
web: www.izzyscubs.com
All creations one-of-a-kind. 'Keep-Sake Bears' made from treasured garments, grandma's fur coat, your wedding dress etc. See website for details.

Hovvig's by Yvonne Graubaek

See you at the Hugglets Winter BearFest
in Kensington February 2008

ROUND ABOUT BEARS
Suffolk, UK
tel: 07785 788307
www.roundaboutbears.co.uk

BEARPATHS
Cleveland Ohio, USA
www.bearpaths.com

HOVVIGs

● J.C.W. BEARS & FURRY FRIENDS
11 Cockerell Close, Pitsea, Basildon, Essex, SS13 1QR
☎ 01268 726558
email: jcwbears@blueyonder.co.uk
web: www.jcwbears.co.uk
Character bears & realistic dogs.

● JAC-Q-LYN BEARS
1 Mere Cottage, School Lane, Marton, Macclesfield, Cheshire, SK11 9HD
☎ 01260 224257
email: jacqlynbears@btinternet.com
web: www.jacqlynbears.com
Original soulful faced wacky mohair bears. One of a kind or small Limited Editions. Trade enquiries welcome.

● JAN'S TIDDY BEARS
75 The Street, Ashtead, Surrey, KT21 1AA
☎ 07889 794637
email: janstiddybears@btinternet.com
web: www.janstiddybears.co.uk
Award winning miniature bear artist. Lovingly designed and hand sewn miniatures by Jan. One to four inches. Commissions taken.

● JASCO BEARS
67 Talbot Street, Southport, Merseyside, PR8 1LU
☎ 01704 539324
email: walmsshei@aol.com
Handmade quality mohair character bears.

● JENNI BEARS
5 Copperfield Road, Poynton, Stockport, Cheshire, SK12 1LX
☎ 01625 877184
email: jennibears@aol.com
Hand sewn mohair artist bears from 3-18". All one off editions and looking for a good home!

JENNYLOVESBENNY BEARS

804/80 Clarendon Street, Southbank, Victoria 3006,
Australia
☎ +61 (0)422 852 236
email: jenny@jennylovesbenny.com
web: www.jennylovesbenny.com
*Please visit my secure online shop for
adorable OOAK ANIME and teddies by
Australian Artist Jenny Lee. Patterns & kits
available.*

JO-ANNE BEARS

20 Wilkin Drive, Tiptree, Essex, CO5 0QP
☎ 01621 815049
email: joanne@jo-annebears.co.uk
web: www.jo-annebears.co.uk
*Award winning artist bears, original designs.
One off bears, small editions. Modern and
traditional, open mouthed, airbrushed, handpainted etc.*

JODIE'S BEARS

Tomoko Suenaga, 3-28-1 Kataseyama, Fujisawa,
Kanagawa, 251-0033, Japan
☎ +81 (0)466 25 1202 Fax: +81 (0)466 27 2260
email: jodie@teddiebear.jp
*Enjoy the fantastic fairy world with my
bears!!*

JOXY BEARS

27 Southgate Gardens, Hornsea, East Yorkshire,
HU18 1RB
☎ 01964 533096
email: jo@joxy.wanadoo.co.uk
web: www.joxybears.co.uk
*Bears, pandas and dogs designed and lov-
ingly hand sewn from tip to toe by Jo.*

JOYBUNNYS ART DESIGNS

33 Trenholme Avenue, Woodside, Bradford, West
Yorkshire, BD6 2NJ
☎ 07971 076259
email: hugs@revjoybunny.fsnet.co.uk
web: www.joybunnysartdesigns.co.uk
*Handcrafted unique bears, novelties and
gifts. All Joybunny originals with a little piece
of nature's beauty in every creation.*

KARIN KRONSTEINER
BEARS - ENVOYS OF MY SOUL

KRENNGASSE 8, A-8010 GRAZ,
AUSTRIA, EUROPE
TEL & FAX: +43 / 316 / 83 91 82
EMAIL: karin.kronsteiner@schule.at
WEB: www.karinkronsteiner.at.tt

JU-BEARY BEARS
Studio 3, Barleylands Craft Village, Barleylands Road,
Billericay, Essex, CM11 2UD
☎ 01268 525775
email: jubearybears@hotmail.co.uk
Exclusively designed mohair collectors bears, pandas and cats by Betty and Julie Guiver. Small limited editions and one offs available.

K M BEARS
by Kerren Morris, 66 Kirklees Drive, Farsley, Pudsey,
West Yorkshire, LS28 5TE
☎ 0113 2192651 Fax: As tel.
email: kerren@kmbears.co.uk
web: www.kmbears.co.uk
Beautiful handmade bears. Commissions undertaken.

KARIN KRONSTEINER BEARS - ENVOYS OF MY SOUL
Krenngasse 8, A-8010, Graz, Austria
☎ +43 (0)316 83 91 82 Fax: As tel.
email: karin.kronsteiner@schule.at
web: www.karinkronsteiner.at.tt
Please see display advertisement.

KAYSBEARS BY KAY STREET
93 Singlewell Road, Gravesend, Kent, DA11 7PU
☎ 01474 351757 Fax: 01322 521746
Award winning miniature bears.

KAYTKINS
9 Ballantyne Road, Rushden, Northamptonshire,
NN10 9FJ
☎ 01933 355782 mob: 07887 877181
email: kiles@totalise.co.uk
Affordable bears made with love.

KAZ BEARS
23 Whinbush Avenue, Allenton, Derby, Derbyshire,
DE24 9DQ
☎ 01332 731948
email: kazbears@ntlworld.com
web: www.kazbears.com
Traditional bears, old looking bears, cute bears, one-offs and small editions. Made from quality mohair, collectable and appealing to all.

KERROWBEARS

by Pat McKerrow, Edinburgh, Scotland
☎ 07971 525377
email: pat@worrek.fsnet.co.uk
web: www.kerrowbears.co.uk
Original, award winning, handcrafted bears made from the finest quality materials. Guaranteed to spread their smiles! Commissions welcome.

KESSEYS BEARS

22 Lon Wen, Park View Estate, Rhyl, Denbighshire, LL18 4JG
☎ 01745 356254
email: susie59uk@yahoo.co.uk
web: www.kesseysbears.com
Unique quirky one of a kind handmade mohair needle felted artist bears & animals.

KEUNS & BEARS

Karin Peire, Smedenstraat 21, Oostende, 8400, Belgium
☎ +32 (0)59 800777
email: karin.peire@skynet.be
web: http://users.skynet.be/keunsandbears
Friendly creatures with a special touch looking for a good home: teabaggies, sptnks, puppies, pandas, rats...you will love them!

KEVINTON BEARS

12 Stanley Street, Caterham, Surrey, CR3 5JY
☎ 07957 333044
email: kevintonbears@aol.com
web: www.kevintonbears.com
Specially designed bears that have a comforting presence and help bring back a positive mood :o)

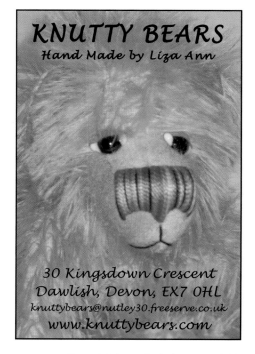

● KINGSTON BEARS

at Heavenly Creations, 43 Christchurch Road, Ringwood, Hampshire, BH24 1DG
☎ 01425 470654 / 470422
email: kingstonbears@aol.com
web: www.kingstonbears.com

One of a kind and small limited edition bears many in antique clothing. Please see display advertisement.

● KNUTTY BEARS

30 Kingsdown Crescent, Dawlish, Devon, EX7 0HL
☎ 01626 863032 web: www.knuttybears.com
email: knuttybears@nutley30.freeserve.co.uk
Hand made alpaca and mohair bears lovingly made by Liza Ann.

● L J BEARS

1 Mead Road, Lymington, Hampshire, SO41 8EP
☎ 01590 676517 Fax: As tel.
email: teddies@ljbears.co.uk
web: www.ljbears.co.uk

Traditional 'hug tested' teddy bears. Bear cats, bunnies and musical bears. Also christening bears and special commissions undertaken. Established 1995.

● LAURIE LOU BEARS

294 Holt Road, Horsford, Norwich, Norfolk, NR10 3EG
☎ 01603 890819
email: lauriewicks@yahoo.co.uk
web: www.laurieloubears.com

Quality homemade mohair collectors bears both traditional and modern. One of a kind bears designed with love and care.

● ELIZABETH LEGGAT - BETH'S BEARS

9 Jamieson Drive, East Kilbride, South Lanarkshire, G74 3EA
☎ 01355 249674
email: elizabeth.leggat@btopenworld.com
web: www.elizabethleggat.co.uk

Edwardian style miniature mohair teddy bears and accessories. Designed and created with the utmost attention to detail.

LILLIAN TRIGG OF ROCHESTER

58 Tern Crescent, Strood, Rochester, Kent, ME2 2RG
☎ 01634 713131
email: linda@lilliantrigg.co.uk
web: www.lilliantrigg.co.uk
Finest quality collectors bears made for the discerning collector.

DE LIN À L'OURS

Christelle Dupré, 7 bis, rue Royer, Messigny et Vantoux 21380, France
☎ +33 (0)3 80 35 46 77
email: contact@lin-ours.com
web: www.lin-ours.com
Traditional hand made Teddy Bears. Original designs, lightly dressed with some accessories and French spirit.

LITTLE ACORNS

24 Mansel Street, Newport, South Wales, NP19 8LA
☎ 01633 271010
email: orphan64@hotmail.com
web: www.littleacorns.org.uk
Bears to treasure by bearsmith Jane Montgomery. Bears to make you smile and melt your heart. 3 to 14 inches.

LITTLE SCRUFFS OF EVESHAM

16-18 High Street, Evesham, Worcestershire, WR11 4HJ
☎ 01386 429002 or 07929 310275
email: littlescruffs@yahoo.co.uk
web: www.miniaturemohairbears.co.uk
Handmade mohair collectors bears. Small vintage style bears, rats and elephants by Jean Grogan. Visitors welcome, please phone first.

LORABEARS

Los Angeles, CA, USA
☎ +1 323 445 3428 Fax: +1 323 655 2613
email: lora@lorabears.com
web: www.lorabears.com
Traditional teddybears, ripened and aged to perfection. Please come visit to meet an old, treasured friend.

WWW.LORABEARS.COM

LOTENI BEARS

Lindy Mullard, 3 Hillside Close, Ormesby St. Margaret, Gt. Yarmouth, Norfolk, NR29 3PY
☎ 01493 731401 (pm/weekend)
Mohair collector bears, fully jointed, lovingly made and each named after the picturesque Norfolk villages amongst which they are born.

LOVE IS IN THE BEAR

72 Lynmere Road, Welling, Kent, DA16 1PA
☎ 020 8304 1412
Handmade traditional bears.

LYNDEE-LOU-BEARS

Farrysthie, Eleanora Drive, Douglas, Isle of Man, IM2 3NN
☎ 01624 616475
email: dee@lyndee-lou-bears.com
web: www.lyndee-lou-bears.com
Hand made collector bears.

MAC BEARS BY CAROL DAVIDSON

36 Fairholme Road, Harrow, Middlesex, HA1 2TN
☎ 020 8863 6192
email: carolscottie@hotmail.com
web: www.macbears.co.uk
Loveable handstitched 5" bears, lead-shot filled.

MADABOUT BEARS

by Lynn Bowie, 18 West End, Dalry, Ayrshire, KA24 5DU
☎ 01294 835432
email: lynn@aldesign.freeserve.co.uk
web: www.aldesign.freeserve.co.uk
Multi nominated award winning artist.

MADELEINE'S MINI BEARS

Madeleine Nelken, 126 Avenue du Général de Gaulle, F-78500 Sartrouville, France
☎ +33 (0)1 39 14 50 86
email: mnelken@aol.com
web: www.madeleineminibears.com
Exquisite miniature bears designed and handcrafted with love 3/4" to 5". One-offs and small limited editions.

MAJACABUS BEARS

Coldharbour Cottage, Back River Drove, Glastonbury, Somerset, BA6 9SZ
☎ 01458 832008
email: carol@majacabusbears.co.uk
web: www.majacabusbears.co.uk
Traditional and character bears, also little friends. Limited editions and one offs. Made with love and care since 1997.

MALU-BEAR

Marie-Luise Barwïtzki, Max-Holder-Str. 8, D-73630 Remshalden, Germany
☎ +49 (0)7151 72769 Fax: As tel.
email: malu@malu-baer.de
web: www.malu-baer.de
Charming old fashioned and cuddly bears. Handmade with love from our own design. One-offs and small limited editions.

MARY MYRTLE MINATURES

web: www.marymyrtleminiatures.co.uk
Award-winning miniature artist bears by Samantha Potter.

MAWSPAWS

The Belfry, 11 Blyth Close, Aylesbury, Buckinghamshire, HP21 8TA
☎ 01296 338338
email: keith@mawspaws.com
web: www.mawspaws.com
Collector bears, pandas, miniatures, personally created by Maureen Batt. One of the UK's most respected artists. Lovely website regularly updated.

MAYPOLE BEARS OF OFFENHAM BY JEAN

Janus Cote, Gibbs Lane, Offenham, Evesham, Hereford & Worcester, WR11 8RR
☎ **01386 48217**
email: **jean@maypolebears.co.uk**
web: **www.maypolebears.co.uk**
Beautifully designed, much sought after. One of a kind jointed bears. Traditional, contemporary. Commissions. Call anytime, a warm welcome awaits.

MEADOWS TEDDY BEARS

26 Gloucester Avenue, Horwich, Bolton, Lancashire, BL6 6NH
☎ 01204 693087
email: stephenjm1@btinternet.com
web: www.ebay.co.uk/bearingifts07
For quality and craftsmanship since 1990. Traditionally made teddy bears lovingly created in top quality mohair by Stephen J. Meadows.

MEGELLES

120 Tinarra Crescent, Kenmore Hills, Queensland 4069, Australia
☎ +61 7 3720 0850
email: ldopking@bigpond.net.au
web: www.megelles.com
Original bears designed and handmade by Lisa Dopking. Bear patterns and kits and stitchery kits featuring Lisa's designs also available.

MELDRUM BEARS

Trelawn Farm, Chapel Hill, Sticker, St. Austell, Cornwall, PL26 7HG
☎ 01726 74499 Fax: As tel.
email: lizmeldrum@fsmail.net
Traditional limited edition collectors bears. Individual commissions & shop exclusives available. For further details please contact Liz Meldrum as above.

MELISSA JAYNE BEARS

14 Castle Court, Castle, Northwich, Cheshire, CW8 1TA
☎ 01606 782183 or 07732 749352 (mob)
email: melissa@melissajaynebears.co.uk
web: www.melissajaynebears.co.uk
Handcrafted mohair teddybears and cats.

MERRYTHOUGHT LTD

Ironbridge, Telford, Shropshire, TF8 7NJ
☎ 01952 433116 Fax: 01952 432054
email: contact@merrythought.co.uk
web: www.merrythought.co.uk

MIDNIGHT BEARS

11 Lower Langley, Great Tey, Colchester, Essex, CO6 1LA
☎ 07864 120945
email: midnightbears@hotmail.com
web: www.midnight-bears.co.uk
Beautiful furry friends, bears, bunnies, dogs and more. Original designs lovingly created by Laura Elder.

MINIKINS BY MAGGIE SPACKMAN

711 Beverly Drive, Bridges of Summerville, Summerville, South Carolina 29485, USA
☎ +1 843 875 2565
email: minikins@sc.rr.com
web: www.maggiesminikins.com
Award winning miniature bears all hand-stitched and fully jointed. Small limited editions and one-offs. Original designs.

MIRKWOOD BEARS

34 Southdown Road, Southdown, Bath, Somerset
☎ 01225 356505
email: sales@mirkwoodbears.co.uk
web: www.mirkwoodbears.co.uk
Hand made bears of distinction. Small limited editions and one off bears with character.

MISS B'S BEARS

The Old School Cottage, 4 Castle Court, School Lane, Holt, Nr Wrexham, Clwyd, Wales, LL13 9YX
☎ 01829 271873
email: bev@missbeesbears.com
web: www.missbeesbears.com
Handmade collectable teddy bears by Bev McConville. Every bear is a one-of-a-kind 'Bundle of Love'.

MISTER BEAR

17 Lord Roberts Avenue, Leigh-on-Sea, Essex, SS9 1ND
☎ 01702 710733 Fax: As tel.
email: jennie@misterbear.net
web: www.misterbear.net
Classical character bears for collectors.

● MUFFTI HUGS

by Christine Boucher, 27 Shenley Road, Bletchely, Milton Keynes, Buckinghamshire
☎ 01908 643679
email: jhbauch@aol.com
Hand made artist bears all one off. Also made to order. Various colours and sizes. Name your own bear.

● NADJA BEARS

Monnikenhofstraat 120, 2040 Berendrecht-Antwerpen, Belgium
☎ +32 (0)3 568 15 15 Fax: As tel.
email: nadia.jacobs@scarlet.be
web: www.nadjabears.be
Old looking bears, waiting to love you. Who wants to give them a home?

● NAMTLOC BEARS

Lynne Coltman, 21 Grasmere Street, Hartlepool, Cleveland, TS26 9AT
☎ 01429 422997
email: namtlocbears@hotmail.com
Original designed handmade bears and crocheted clothes for both bears and dolls. Commissions welcome. See Bear Gallery.

● NARNIE BEARS

by Christine Howe, 1 Taylors Croft, Main Road, Authorpe, Louth, Lincolnshire, LN11 8PQ
☎ 07903 082630 / 01507 451380
Hand sewn teddies. Commissions welcome. Payment in instalments discussed. One of a kind designs. Love is a bear always there.

● NETTY'S BEARS

16 Ormonde Avenue, Epsom, Surrey, KT19 9EP
☎ 01372 813558
email: netty.paterson@ntlworld.com
web: www.jannettysbears.co.uk
See entry under JanNetty's Bears.

● NOBODYS BEAR

3 Hillside Meadows, Foxhole, St Austell, Cornwall, PL26 7TA
☎ 01726 824136
email: nobodysbear@hotmail.co.uk
web: www.nobodysbear.eu
A noBodys Bear needs somebody beautiful. One off designs by artist Chrissy.

● NORMANDY BEARS

Village de la Rivière, 50620 St Fromond, France
☎ +33 (0)2 33 55 98 61 Fax: As tel.
email: vicki.philip@wanadoo.fr
Collectors bears with French flair. Handcrafted by Vicki Philip in Normandy. One of a kind. Commissions welcome.

● OKIDOKI ORIGINAL

Pistolvägen 6, 22649 Lund, Sweden
☎ +46 (0)46 142089 or (0)46 133820
Fax: +46 (0)46 133820
email: kajsa.lindstrom@telia.com
web: www.okidokioriginal.com
Colourful collection of one-off animals in washed wool. Bears, rabbits, duckies, pigs, dogs and more - all dressed up to go!

● OOPS! PARDON ME, BEARS!

12 Portmarnock Way, Grantham, Lincolnshire, NG31 9FL
☎ 01476 563599
email: eileen.wood@mail.bta.com
web: http://eileenwood.bta.com/oops
Artist bears by Eileen Woods.

● ORCHARD BEARS

2 Old Heatherdene Cottages, Common Road, Great Kingshill, High Wycombe, Buckinghamshire, HP15 6EZ
☎ 01494 717501
email: hayley@orchardbears.com
web: www.orchardbears.com
Traditional mohair bears designed and made by Hayley Orchard. Mail order available, send sae for details or see website.

● ORIGINAL RICA-BEAR®

Ulrike and Claude Charles, Friesenstr. 5, 32760 Detmold, Germany
☎ +49 (0)5231 59750 Fax: +49 (0)5231 580018
email: mail@rica-bear.de
web: www.rica-bear.de
Traditional collectors bears designed and handmade by Ulrike and Claude Charles. Small limited editions and one-offs.

OUT OF THE WOODS©
1 Colegate Barn Cottages, Coopers Hill Road, Nutfield, Surrey, RH1 4HX
☎ 01737 821218
email: samsalter1@aol.com
Award winning mohair bears each beautifully dressed. Send SAE for details.

PAM HOWELLS
39 Frognall, Deeping St James, Peterborough, Cambridgeshire, PE6 8RR
☎ 01778 344152
Quality traditional teddy bears. Hand crafted from the finest mohair. Limited edition collectors' bears and award winning exclusive soft toys.

PANDA JAK BEARS
Belisker, Brickens, Claremorris, Co Mayo, Ireland
☎ +353 (0)94 938 0962
email: amandaj.ellis@hotmail.co.uk
Traditional bears lovingly created in the emerald isle by Amanda.

PAW PRINTS OF STAFFORDSHIRE
4 Campian Way, Norton, Stoke on Trent, Staffordshire, ST6 8FA
☎ 01782 537315
email: cjkeen@pawprints.org.uk
web: www.pawprints.org.uk
Beautiful limited edition bears.

PCBANGLES
79 Grenville Road, Aylesbury, Buckinghamshire, HP21 8ET
☎ 07931 216695 Fax: 01296 483664
email: pcbangles@tiscali.co.uk
web: www.pcbangles.co.uk
Cheeky mohair bears in a rainbow of colours. OOAK and small Limited Editions available. Housetrained and huggable!

LOUISE PEERS
2 The Lawns, Wilmslow, Cheshire, SK9 6EB
☎ 01625 527917 Fax: As tel.
email: ldpeers@btinternet.com
web: www.louisepeers.blogspot.com
Award winning miniature bears. Please send £2.50 for catalogue of new bears or visit my web page for available bears.

PENNBEARY
23 Priors Walk, St Johns Priory, Lechlade, Gloucestershire, GL7 3HR
☎ 01367 252809
email: pennbeary@tiscali.co.uk
Award-winning mohair bears, hand stitched by Penny Roberts. One-offs and small limited editions. £1.50 for photographs and details.

PENNY BUNN BEARS
Pathways, Middle Street, Eastington, Stonehouse, Gloucestershire, GL10 3BB
☎ 01453 828060 Fax: As tel.
email: bearsbyNKW@aol.com
web: www.pennybunnbears.co.uk
Beautiful miniature bears for collectors.

NICOLA PERKINS
Ivy Cottage, Leycet Lane, Madeley Heath, Crewe, Cheshire, CW3 9LS
☎ 01782 751077
email: nicola@timcoggins.orangehome.co.uk
Vintage style one of a kind miniature bears. Dressed using antique and vintage trimmings and fabrics. Commissions undertaken.

Bears by Angela Jardine

**Hand dyed mohair bears
with oodles of character and
cuddle power**

One of a kind

Limited Editions

www.pcbangles.co.uk
email: pcbangles@tiscali.co.uk
tel: 07931 216695

● **PERTINAX BEARS**
email: pertinaxbears@yahoo.co.uk
web: www.pertinaxbears.co.uk
Please see display advertisement.

● **PETAL ORIGINALS**
by Elaine Goodhand, 29 Lower Hill Road, Epsom,
Surrey, KT19 8LS
☎ 01372 724386
email: petalbears@aol.com
Special Gollies - commissions accepted.

● **PICK-ME BEARS**
Zellerhornstr. 43, 81549 Munich, Germany
☎ +49 (0)89 6924102
email: robena@pick-me-bears.com
web: www.pick-me-bears.com
*Unique tribe of bears that live in the land of
Willmagoo. All are handcrafted and come
with a story or poem.*

THE PIECE PARADE

7405 Laketree Drive, Raleigh, NC 27615, USA
☎ +1 919 870 1881
email: gbrame@pieceparade.com
web: www.pieceparade.com
Junkyard sprites, 'bears&boxes', & 3-12 inch teddies created with care by ginger brame. Exclusive internet shows semi-annually.

PIJANGI BEARS

Birgitte Nemler, Egelundsvej 73, Stroeby Egede, 4600 Koege, Denmark
☎ +45 5626 8320
email: pijangi@tdcadsl.dk
web: www.pijangibears.dk
Beautiful handmade artist bears in mohair or synthetic. Best quality. Sweet faces with soulful glass eyes. Wired ears for possibilities.

PIPALUCK BEARS

16 Beechfield Road, Welwyn Garden City, Hertfordshire, AL7 3RF
☎ 07966 162650
email: april@pipaluck.co.uk
web: www.pipaluck.co.uk
Handmade bears of original design by April Yelland, funky and fun, full of character and made with love. Commissions welcome.

PIPEDREAM BEARS

28 Chiltern Drive, Woodsmoor, Stockport, Cheshire, SK2 7BE
☎ 0161 285 8254
email: r.cardey@ntlworld.com
web: www.bearsandpugs.com
Magical fairy bears made from pipecleaners featuring handmade toadstools. Also miniature mohair bears handmade by Jan Cardey and Sue Heap.

PIPKINS BEARS

4 Cyclamen Close, Branston, Staffordshire, DE14 3FJ
email: pip8767@hotmail.com
web: www.pipkinsbears.com
Quality traditional collectors bears designed and created by award-winning artist, Jane Powell. Range includes Miniatures, Elves and Faerie Bears.

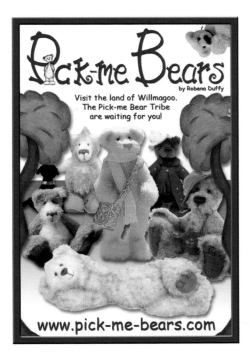

● PIPPAWICKS

4 Knoll Rise, St. Leonards-On-Sea, East Sussex,
TN38 0NT
☎ 01424 428676
*Hand crafted bears and other curious
creatures by Dawn.*

● PIXEL'S BEARS

**Lea Holme, Whiteway Head Lane, Knowbury,
Ludlow, Shropshire, SY8 3EL**
☎ **01584 890472**
email: info@pixelsbears.com
web: www.pixelsbears.com
*High quality handmade collectable award
winning artist bears. One off's and small
limited editions. Commissions welcome.
See website for full details.*

● POGMEAR BEARS

8 Duporth Bay, St Austell, Cornwall, PL26 6AG
☎ 07730 788581
*Limited edition handmade mohair bears for
collectors.*

● PUMPKIN & PICKLE BEARS

East Sussex
☎ 01892 652706
email: pumpkinandpickle@hotmail.co.uk
web: www.pumpkinandpickle.co.uk
*OOAK bears made by Gemma McKenzie
using mohair and quality plush. Sizes range
from 2-17".*

● PUZZLE BEARS

61 Send Road, Send, Nr Woking, Surrey, GU23 7EU
☎ **01483 224524**
email: anitaweller@puzzlebears.fsnet.co.uk
web: www.puzzlebears.com
*Handmade collectors mohair bears,
designed by Anita Weller, traditional,
themed character and miniature bears
made to order.*

● PYWACKET TEDDIES

Lin Grant, 75 Froxfield Road, West Leigh, Havant,
Hampshire, PO9 5PW
☎ 023 9245 2266   Fax: As tel.
Quality bears and other animals.

SUE QUINN

Hunter House, 7 Hunter Street, Paisley, Renfrewshire, PA1 1DN, Scotland

☎ 0141 887 9916 Fax: 01505 702163

email: sue@bearsbysuequinn.co.uk

web: www.bearsbysuequinn.co.uk

Bears by Sue Quinn. Limited edition traditional jointed bears, dressed or undressed, in pure mohair and other quality fabrics.

THE RABBIT MAKER

Mountain Ash, 140 Chapel Road, Hesketh Bank, Preston, Lancashire, PR4 6RY

☎ 01772 811254

email: shelly@therabbitmaker.com

web: www.therabbitmaker.com

Rabbit lovers stop here! Shelly specializes in mohair and alpaca rabbits, dressed in beautifully designed outfits. Please see display advert.

RAMSHACKLE BEARS

'Ramshackle Cottage', 14 West Street, Shoreham-by-Sea, W Sussex, BN43 5WG

☎ 01273 454746

Handmade mohair bears and restorations.

ANNETTE RAUCH

Neuhäuser Straße 42, 98701, Grossbreitenbach, Germany

☎ +49 (0)36781 40363 Fax: +49 (0)36781 29470

email: annette.rauch@t-online.de

web: www.annette-rauch.com

Handmade bears and animals from natural materials whose personal information will always be found on their bottoms.

READY TEDI GO!

102 Priory Way, Haywards Heath, West Sussex, RH16 3NP

☎ 01444 413487

Collectable bears by Irene Wright.

RED OR TED

Wall Hill Cottage, 3 Junction Road, Leek, Staffordshire, ST13 5QL

☎ 07875 498763

email: lesley@redorted.co.uk

web: www.redorted.co.uk

Unique handmade artist bears, wannabe bears and bear clothes. Vintage bears from around the world.

REMEM-BEAR ARTIST BEARS

Braeside, 3 Mineral Terrace, Foxdale, Isle of Man, IM4 3EY

☎ 07624 489906

email: remembear@yahoo.com

web: www.remembear.com

OOAK traditionally antique style and also funky, wacky bears. Also mohair, kits, patterns and supplies.

RHIW VALLEY BEARS

2 Trem Hirnant, Manafon, Welshpool, Powys, SY21 8BX

☎ 01686 650883

email: margery.youden@virgin.net

Handmade bears by Marge.

pipedream bears

tel 01612858254 / 01614566142
email r.cardey@ntlworld.com

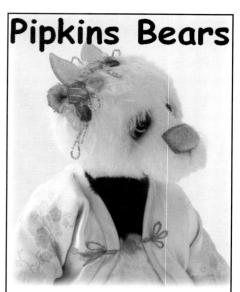

Pipkins Bears

Designed & Created By Jane Powell
www.pipkinsbears.com
pip8767@hotmail.com

The Rabbit Maker

Traditional style rabbits in designer outfits.

www.therabbitmaker.com

Tel: 01772 811254

● ROBIN RIVE BEARS
Countrylife New Zealand Ltd, 2nd floor, 145-157 St John Street, London, EC1V 4PY
☎ 0121 288 0548
email: briguk@robinrive.com
web: www.robinrive.com
International award-winning New Zealand bear-artist Robin Rive designs nostalgic soft collectibles including limited edition fully jointed mohair teddys and gollys.

● ROSIE'S ATTIC
'The Apple Loft', Drayton Manor, Drayton, Somerset, TA10 0LL
☎ 07776 191960
email: rosieintheattic@yahoo.co.uk
web: www.rosiesattic.co.uk
Handmade country bears, dolls and accessories.

● ROWAN BEARS
147 Singleton Crescent, Goring-By-Sea, Worthing, West Sussex, BN12 5DJ
☎ 01903 240467 mobile 07952 149578
email: rowanbears@hotmail.co.uk
web: www.rowanbears.co.uk
Stunning bears, realistic Guinea pigs and Border Terriers. All unique designs handmade in Schulte mohair or alpaca.

● RUBEN BEARS
164 Cutenhoe Road, Luton, Bedfordshire, LU1 3NF
☎ 01582 731544
email: rubenbears@aol.com
Lovable bears requiring loving homes.

● RUNNING BEAR COMPANY
Eisinghausener Str. 309, 26789 Leer, Germany
☎ +49 (0)491 912 1526 Fax: +49 (0)491 940 7264
email: runningbearco@aol.com
web: www.runningbearcompany.de
Bears to make you smile.

● SAINT BEAR
Nagasaki, Japan
email: saintbear3@nifty.com
web: http://homepage3.nifty.com/saint/
Award winning teddy bears hand-made by Kaeko Hayashida. 'I want to make bears that will stay in your heart'.

● SALLY ANNE BEARS

19 Abingdon Avenue, Doddington Park, Lincoln, LN6 3LB
☎ 01522 509329
email: sanray55@talktalk.net
web: www.sallyannebears.co.uk
Award-winning dressed and undressed collectable bears by Sandra Hobbs.

● SALLY B BEARS

☎ email: salandbaz@hotmail.com
web: www.sally-b-bears.co.uk
Award winning OOAK artist bears (mainly miniatures), designed and handmade with great care and attention to detail by Sally Mathew.

● SALLY B GOLLIES

12 Bridges Close, Wokingham, Berks, RG41 3XL
☎ 0118 9775464 Fax: 0118 9773228
email: zarir@btinternet.com
Distinctive, individual gollies often with subjects of well known characters from stage, screen or history. Always depicted kindly and humourously.

PYWACKET TEDDIES

TRADITIONAL AND CHARACTER BEARS, PANDAS, ELEPHANTS, CATS, WABBITS, RATS, MICE, BADGERS, HEDGEHOGS, FOXES and 'BIGFOOT' by LIN GRANT

75 FROXFIELD ROAD, WEST LEIGH, HAVANT, HAMPSHIRE, ENGLAND PO9 5PW TEL/FAX 023 92452266

www.bearsbysuequinn.co.uk

Bears by SUE QUINN

Limited Editions
Shop Exclusives
One-off Designs

Hunter House,
7 Hunter Street, Paisley,
Renfrewshire, Scotland,
PA1 1DN
Tel: 0141 887 9916
Fax: 01505 702163
sue@bearsbysuequinn.co.uk

Saint Bear

Kaeko Hayashida
http://homepage3.nifty.com/saint/
email: saintbear3@nifty.com

● SAMBROOK BEARS
29 Robertson Drive, Wickford, Essex, SS12 9QH
☎ 01268 562163
email: mandy@sambrookbears.co.uk
web: www.sambrookbears.co.uk
*Original and OOAK miniature bears hand
crafted with great care and attention to
ensure each creation is perfectly adorable.*

● SARAH'S BEARS OF CAMBRIDGE
62 Mill Lane, Impington, Cambridge, Cambridgeshire,
CB4 9HS
☎ 01223 566960
email: sarahsbears@ntlworld.com
web: www.sarahsbearsofcambridge.com
*Traditional, fully jointed mohair bears hand-
made by Sarah Cox. One-offs, small editions
and exclusive Cambridge University bears.*

● SARAH'S BRUINS
24 Victoria Road, Wisbech, Cambs, PE13 2QL
☎ 01945 461257
email: sarahsbruins@aol.com
web: www.sarahsbruins.co.uk
*One of a kind, loveable, handstitched bears
(bunnies too!). See website for new address!*

● SCRUFFIE BEARS BY SUSAN PRYCE
19 Parkfield Road, Broughton, Nr Chester, Flintshire,
CH4 0SE
☎ 01244 534724
email: scruffiebears@aol.com
web: www.scruffiebears.com
*Mohair artist bears, mainly one of a kind with
each bear having their own personality.*

● SCRUFFY BEARS
Flat 6, 57 Norfolk Road, Littlehampton, West Sussex,
BN17 5HE
☎ 01903 734865
*Big bears, small bears. Bears handsewn with
love just waiting to come home with you.*

● SCRUMPY BEARS
Abbotswood, Hanning Road, Horton, Ilminster,
Somerset, TA19 9QH
☎ 01460 52002
email: scrumpybear12@aol.com
Please see display advertisement.

● SEASHORE BEARS
20 Tweed Street, Ayr, Ayrshire, KA8 9JD
☎ 01292 288252
email: jocelyn.gough@seashorebears.co.uk
web: www.seashorebears.co.uk
*Hand made collectors bears by Jocelyn
Gough. All one of a kind. Commissions welcome. Please view my website.*

● SHANTOCK BEARS
22 Downside, Hemel Hempstead, Herts, HP2 5PY
☎ 01442 260486
email: shantockbears@tiscali.co.uk
web: www.shantockbears.com
Traditional, themed and pretty bears.

SHEBOB BEARS

7 Cottage Place, Copthorne, Crawley, Sussex, RH10 3LF

☎ 01342 714568

email: sheila.tester@tesco.net

Lovingly handcrafted collectors bears with personality by Sheila Tester. See picture in Bear Gallery. Phone or email for full details.

JULIE SHEPHERD

The Old School Cottage, Woolbeding, Midhurst, West Sussex, GU29 0QB

☎ 01730 810878

email: julie@julieshepherd.com

web: www.julieshepherd.com

Bears, bunnies and pandas with kind and gentle faces. Designed and lovingly crafted by award winning artist. Photos available.

SCRUMPYBEARS
Original Handmade Miniature Bears

Abbotswood, Hanning Rd, Horton, Ilminster, Somerset, TA19 9QH
Tel: 01460 52002 Email: scrumpybear12@aol.com

● SHULTZ CHARACTERS
by Paula Strethill-Smith, 4 Little Park Mansions, Titchfield Lane, Wickham, Hampshire, PO17 5PD
☎ 01329 834681 Fax: As tel.
email: p.strethillsmith@btconnect.com
web: www.paulastrethill-smith.com
Created by Paula Strethill-Smith, international award winning artist. Vintage style miniature teddy bears, dogs, mice, rabbits and other characters.

● SMILEY RILEY - BEARS BY ANJI
55 Garners Lane, Stockport, Cheshire, SK3 8SD
email: anjiriley@ntlworld.com
Bears to make you smile! One-off colourful button jointed bears around 4 inches. Email for a picture or two.

● SNAZZY GOLLYS
60 Arundel Road, Littlehampton, West Sussex, BN17 7DF
☎ 01903 721070
email: gollyhouse@hotmail.com
Traditional and modern styles. One offs and small limited editions. Restoration service for overloved gollys. SAE or email for details.

● SOUTHWAY BEARS
11 Stephen Martin Gardens, Fordingbridge, Hampshire, SP6 1RF
☎ 01425 654768 Fax: As tel.
email: southwaybears@hotmail.com
web: www.southwaybears.co.uk
Beautiful mohair bears. Commissions welcomed. Sue is a member of the British Toymakers Guild.

● SPRINGER BEARS
26 Devonshire Avenue, Ripley, Derbyshire, DE5 3SS
☎ 01773 748093
email: springerbears@aol.com
Original bears made with love.

● STANLEY BEARS
Rosengren Lane, Stanley, Victoria 3747, Australia
☎ +61 (0)3 5728 6623
email: eunice@stanleybears.com.au
web: www.stanleybears.com.au
I am Eunice Eiseman, a professional teddy bear artist (established 1990) specialising in exclusive teddies for discerning collectors worldwide.

● STARLITE BEARS
32 Robertson Avenue
☎ 07802 568685
email: starlite_bears@yahoo.co.uk
web: www.starlitebears.co.uk
Beautiful, hand made OOAK mini/miniature bears (2.5" to 6"). Each little creation has a unique, charming personality!

● MARGARETE STEIFF GMBH
Richard Steiff Strasse 4, D-89537 Giengen/Brenz, Germany
☎ +49 (0)7322 131-1 Fax: +49 (0)7322 131-2 66
web: www.steiff-club.de
Richard Steiff invented the world's first Teddy bear in 1902.

STEIFF UK

Astra House, The Common, Cranleigh, Surrey, GU6 8RZ
☎ 01483 266643 Fax: 01483 266650
email: leyla.maniera@steiff.com
Visit www.steiff-club.de to find your nearest stockist.

STUDIO 44

7 High Street, Donington, Spalding, Lincolnshire, PE11 4TA
☎ **01775 820429**
email: studio44@btinternet.com
web: www.studio44bears.com
Collectors bears by Dorothy and Michael Short. Individually designed characters hand crafted in traditional and modern materials.

TAMERTON TEDDYS

44 Rollis Park Road, Oreston, Plymouth, Devon, PL9 7LY
☎ 01752 480656
email: berylwhite@blueyonder.co.uk
Collectors bears by Beryl White.

TEACHERS PETS

81 Queens Road, Bury St Edmunds, Suffolk, IP33 3EW
☎ 01284 704253
email: marilyn.asbridge@btopenworld.com
web: www.teacherspetsonline.co.uk
Handsewn collector's bears, all individuals. Made with care from mohair or alpaca. Each has a gold star for being good!

TEDDY BEARS UK

93 Downfield Road, Cheshunt, Hertfordshire, EN8 8SR
☎ 01992 309282
email: sheilafrances@ntlworld.com
web: www.teddybears.uk.com
One of a kind bears, on a traditional theme, some dressed for fun. Hand made with love by Sheila Frances.

TEDI ENFYS

39 Keene Ave, Rogerstone, Newport, S Wales, NP10 9DF
☎ 01633 780247
Teddies with a smile. Handmade traditional and modern style originally designed bears. Wide variety of sizes and mohairs. Also gollies.

TEDI TY COED

Forest Lodge, Treherbert, Treorchy, R.C.T., CF42 5PH
☎ 01443 776031
web: www.teditycoed.co.uk
Quality original handmade mohair bears.

TEDS OF THE RIVERBANK

'Riverbank', 2 Bohemia Cottages, Stalybridge, Cheshire, SK15 1JY
☎ 0161 303 0011
email: tedsoftheriverbank@btopenworld.com
web: www.tedsoftheriverbank.com
Artist teds for all tastes.

www.julieshepherd.com

"Artist Teds for all Tastes"
by Barbara Ann Harding

Visitors welcome to our small bear and toy
museum – please ring first!
Commissions and renovations undertaken.

"Riverbank", 2 Bohemia Cottages,
Stalybridge Cheshire SK15 1JY
Tel: 0161 303 0011
email: tedsoftheriverbank@btopenworld.com
www.tedsoftheriverbank.com

● TEENY BEARS
11 Sparsholt Road, Weston, Southampton, Hants,
SO19 9NH
☎ 02380 446356
email: tina@teenybears.co.uk
web: www.teenybears.co.uk
Designed and hand made with love by Tina.

● TEWIN'S BRUINS
16 Lower Green, Tewin, Welwyn, Hertfordshire,
AL6 0LB
☎ 01438 718700 Fax: 01438 840411
email: tbrand@talk21.com
*Terry Brand (BA) handmade collector bears,
rabbits, dogs, cats, mice, gollies etc...*

● THE BEAR NECESSITIES - KNARF-BEARS
Groeninge 23, 8000 Brugge, Belgium
☎ +32 (0)5034 1027 Fax: +32 (0)5034 1027
email: info@thebearnecessities.be
web: www.thebearnecessities.be
*Artist bears by Maria Devlieghere.
Beautiful original artist collector's bears
from around the world. Unique Knarf
Bears - limited editions.*

● THE TEDDY SHOP
93 Downfield Road, Cheshunt, Hertfordshire, EN8 8SR
☎ 01992 309282
email: sheilafrances@ntlworld.com
web: www.the-teddy-shop.co.uk
*Traditional teddies hand made with mohair
and plush. Knitted teddies and clothing.
Teddy patterns. teddy themed items. By
Sheila Frances.*

● THE THING ABOUT BEARS
The Olde Bear Workshop, 163 Mongeham Road,
Great Mongeham, Deal, Kent, CT14 9LL
☎ 01304 369253
email: sam@thethingaboutbears.com
web: www.thethingaboutbears.com
*Traditional mohair artist bears by Sam
Glanville. One of a kind. Worldwide delivery.
Visit my website today.*

● ELIZABETH THOMPSON

12 Briar Thicket, Woodstock, Oxfordshire, OX20 1NT
☎ 01993 811915
email: thompelix@aol.com
High quality mohair and synthetic bears. Stock or personalised to order. For collectors and children.

● THREADTEDS

De Braak 11, 5963 BA Horst, Netherlands
☎ +31 (0)77 3984960
email: threadteds@xs4all.nl
web: www.threadteds.com
Original traditional, crochet, needle felted and crofelt artist collectables. Offering thread bear patterns, book, kits, mini fabric and supplies!

● THREE O'CLOCK BEARS

27 Knoll Drive, Styvechale, Coventry, West Midlands, CV3 5BU
☎ 024 7641 6654 Fax: As tel.
email: jenny@threeoclockbears.com
web: www.threeoclockbears.com
Sweet faced individually made bears and friends designed and stitched by Jenny Johnson. Enquiries most welcome.

● TILLINGTON BEARS

13 Hurdles Way, Duxford, Cambridge, CB22 4PA
☎ 01223 837701
email: tilly@tillingtonbears.co.uk
web: www.tillingtonbears.co.uk
Call or email Tilly today, or look at our website to see a unique range of mohair bears with style.

Hugglets PUBLISHING

● TINY TEDDIES BY ANN
3 Cheriton Drive, Thornhill, Cardiff, South Glamorgan, CF14 9DF
☎ 029 2075 3133 email: ann@tinyteddiesbyann.co.uk
web: www.tinyteddiesbyann.co.uk
Miniatures a speciality. One-off handsewn unique designs 1-14 ins in mohair, cashmere, knitted silk thread. Miniature kits, fabrics, accessories available.

● TINYBEAR
Tina Jensen, Gl. Hareskovvej 311, 1, 3500 Vaerlose, Denmark
☎ +45 4444 1898
email: tinybear@tinybear.dk
web: www.tinybear.dk
Tiny hand made bears with souls. Original designs. Made by Danish artist Tina Jensen.

● TOGGLE TEDDIES
25 Laund Avenue, Belper, Derbyshire, DE56 1FL
☎ 01773 824258
email: wendi@toggleteddies.co.uk
web: www.toggleteddies.co.uk
Beautifully handcrafted original designer bears and raggedy dolls by Artist Wendi Walker.

● TONNIBEARS
by Marjan Jorritsma, de Veldkamp 1, 9461 PA Gieten, Netherlands
☎ +31 592 262854 Fax: As tel.
email: bears@tonnibears.nl
web: www.tonnibears.nl
Celebrating my 14th year of award winning one-of-a-kind and small edition bears and other animals. Also crosstitch kits and patterns.

● TOP 'N' TAIL TEDDY BEARS
82 Downs Road, Walmer, Deal, Kent, CT14 7TB
☎ 01304 363040
email: info@topntail.com web: www.topntail.com
Traditional bears with nostalgic character. Made to a very high standard with much fine detail from 7" up to 24".

● TORQUAY TEDDIES
27 Shetland Close, Torquay, Devon, TQ2 7BH
☎ 07867 863664
email: torquay.teddies@gmail.com
One of a kind bears up to 10" tall in mohair and velvet. Bears to order or write for details.

● TOYS, STUFFED AND HANDMADE BY SUSAN
Proprietor: Susan Mansfield-Jones, 23 Sabrina Drive, Toronto, Ontario, M9R 2J4, Canada
☎ +1 416 242 6446
Soft: mohair acrylic or polyfibre material. Stuffed: buckshot, plastic pellets, polyester & foam. Sculpture: 10cms-100cms height. Sculptures may include growler/musicbox.

● TRENDLE INTERNATIONAL LTD
PO Box 3, Williton, Taunton, Somerset, TA4 4YU
☎ 01984 656825
email: mail@trendle.com web: www.trendle.com
Please see colour display advertisement.

● TWILIGHT TEDS
by Tracey James, 37 Roeburn Way, Penketh, Cheshire, WA5 2PF
☎ 01925 725084
email: twilight_teds@hotmail.com
web: www.twilight-teds.co.uk
British Bear Artist Awards finalist 2003, 2004 and 2005. Artist bears, pandas, bunnies and gollies. Entirely hand stitched, 'one-off' exclusives.

VALEWOOD BEARS

15 Vale Grove, Queensbury, Bradford, West Yorkshire, BD13 2QR
☎ 01274 883783
email: queens@valewood.fsnet.co.uk
web: www.valewoodbears.co.uk
Unique handcrafted collector bears and bunnies. Also bear clothes.

VERA BEARS

19, 14th Street, 2193 Parkhurst, Johannesburg, South Africa
☎ +27 (0)11 788 3107 Fax: As tel.
email: vera@verabears.com web: www.verabears.com
Miniature teddy bears designed and handmade with love by Vera Matic in mohair and other materials. 1-5 inches.

VERY I BEARS

3 Liskeard Lodge, Tupwood Lane, Caterham, CR3 6DN
☎ 07789 865920 web: www.veryibears.co.uk
email: goldfish@aquarium99.freeserve.co.uk
One of a kind hand made bears and bunnies with unique embroidered footpads by Victoria Penney.

WARREN BEARS

4 Goddington Lane, Orpington, Kent, BR6 9DS
☎ 01689 871420
email: melanie@warrenbears.co.uk
web: www.warrenbears.co.uk
Distinctive mohair and alpaca bears with sweet faces.

WELLWOOD BEARS

Ruth Dickinson, 46 Wellwood, Llanedeyrn, Cardiff, South Glamorgan, CF23 9JQ
☎ 029 2073 6610
email: ruth@wellwoodbears.freeserve.co.uk
web: www.wellwoodbears.com
Collectors bears. One offs, small limited editions. Available at fairs, shops or direct. See my website for bears and information.

● WESTIE BEARS

12 Norfolk Road, Horsham, West Sussex, RH12 1BZ
☎ 01403 241381 Fax: As tel.
email: andy@westiebears.com
web: www.westiebears.com

Award winning mini bears and other critters. Wild wacky punky bears and traditional mini huggers. Bespoke orders taken.

● WHITTLE-LE-WOODS BEARS

23 Leinster Street, Farnworth, Bolton, Lancashire, BL4 9HS
☎ 01204 706831 Fax: As tel.
email: arnie.witt@ntlworld.com

Traditional, limited edition mohair artist bears. Unique designs handcrafted by the artist. Meet our teddies at the Hugglets shows.

WHITTLE-LE-WOODS BEARS

TRADITIONAL LIMITED EDITION TEDDY BEARS FOR THE DISCERNING COLLECTOR, SEE OUR LISTING FOR DETAILS.
CONTACT- IRENE & MIKE WHITTLE TEL 01204 706831

● WINKLEMOOR BEARS
11 Newport Road, Cwmcarn, Crosskeys, Newport, Gwent, NP11 7NE
☎ 01495 244528 mob: 07973 383128
email: elaine@winklemoor.co.uk
web: www.winklemoor.co.uk
Hand crafted collectors bears and friends. Nearly all one of a kind. A Winklemoor Bear always listens, never tells.

● WISHING WELL BEARS
The Bear Emporium, Ridgeway Craft Centre, Ridgeway, Nr Sheffield, Derbyshire, S12 3XR
☎ 0114 248 2010
web: www.bear-emporium.com
Exquisite handcrafted lovable character bears. Commissions welcome.

● WOODGATE BEARS
8 Woodgate Meadow, Plumpton Green, Lewes, E. Sussex, BN7 3BD
☎ 01273 891665
email: suewhittaker132@btinternet.com
web: www.woodgatebears.co.uk
Handmade mohair and alpaca bears.

● WOODLAND TEDDIES
Rita Harwood, 5 Mildenhall Road, Loughborough, Leicestershire, LE11 4SN
☎ 01509 267597 mob: 07973 821816
email: rita@woodlandteddies.com
web: www.woodlandteddies.com
From Realistic to Wildly OTT, handsewn, hand dyed and deliciously original critters by Teddy Bear Scene's Creative Editor, Rita Harwood.

● WOODROW BEARS
19 Woodland View, Rogiet, Monmouthshire, NP26 3SY
☎ 01291 421369
email: beryl@stopgate.fslife.co.uk
web: www.woodrowbears.co.uk
Handmade dressed and natural bears, mostly one offs. We are at Cirencester Corn Hall first and third Saturday every month.

● WOODVILLE BEARS
86 Bernard Street, Woodville, Swadlincote, Derbyshire, DE11 8BY
☎ 01283 221829
email: val-bears@hotmail.co.uk
Traditional handmade mohair collectors bears.

● YESTERDAY'S CHILDREN
Mill House, Mill Lane, St. Ive's Cross, Sutton St. James, Nr Spalding, Lincolnshire, PE12 0EJ
☎ 01945 440466
Individually designed, collectable, completely hand sewn, no order too small - maximum five of one design, many fabrics and sizes.

END

Website Index

A Hitchcock Bear	-	www.ahitchcockbear.com
ABC	-	www.geocities.com/artist_bears
Abracadabra Teddy Bears	-	www.abracadabra-teddies.com
Actually Bears by Jackie	-	www.actuallybearsbyjackie.co.uk
Admiral Bears Supplies	-	www.admiral-bears.com
Alexander Bears	-	www.freewebs.com/alexanderbears
All Bear	-	www.allbear.co.uk
All Things Beary	-	www.allbeary.com
All You Can Bear	-	www.allyoucanbear.com
Allsorts of bears	-	www.allsortsofbears.com
Always Bearing in Mind	-	www.alwaysbearinginmind.co.uk
AM Bears	-	www.ambears.co.uk
Amanda's Honey Pot Bears	-	www.honeypotbears.com
AngieBears	-	www.angiebears.net
Ann Made Bears	-	www.ann-made-bears.co.uk
Ann_Knits 4 Bears	-	www.knits4bears.co.uk
Anna Koetse's Bears	-	www.annakoetse.com
Apple Pie House Ltd	-	www.applepiehouse.com
Arctophilia	-	www.arctophilia.com
Arundel Teddy Bears	-	www.arundelteddybears.co.uk
Ashby Bears & Collectables	-	www.ashbybears.com
Ashwood Nurseries Gift Shop	-	www.ashwoodnurseries.com
Asquiths	-	www.asquiths.com
Atlantic Bears	-	www.atlanticbears.co.uk
Aurorabearealis	-	www.aurorabearealis.co.uk
B-Bears And Gifts	-	www.BearsAndGifts.com.au
Ba's Bears	-	www.basbears.com
Bacton Bears	-	www.bactonbears.co.uk
Baggaley Bears	-	www.freewebs.com/baggaleybears
Balu Bears	-	www.balu-baer.de
Barbara-Ann Bears	-	www.barbara-annbears.com
Bärenboutique	-	www.baerenboutique.de
Bärenhäusl - Ositos®-Bären	-	www.ositos-baeren.de
Barling Bears	-	www.barlingbears.co.uk
Barrel Bears	-	www.barrelbears.co.uk
Barron Bears	-	www.barronteddybears.com
Baybee Bears	-	www.baybeebears.piczo.com
Bear Bahoochie	-	www.bearbahoochie.co.uk
Bear Basics	-	www.bearbasics.co.uk
Bear Bits	-	www.bearbits.com
Bear Club, The	-	www.thebearclub.co.uk
Bear Crazee	-	www.bearcrazee.com
Bear Emporium, The	-	www.bear-emporium.com

Bear Garden, The	- www.beargarden.co.uk
Bear Huggery, The	- www.thebearhuggery.co.uk
Bear It In Mind	- www.bearitinmind.com
Bear Patch, The	- www.thebearpatch.co.uk
Bear Paths	- www.bearpaths.com
Bear Pawtraits	- www.bearpawtraits.com
Bear Shop, Colchester, The	- www.bearshops.co.uk
Bear Supplies Company	- www.bearsupplies.co.uk
Bear Treasures by Melanie Jayne	- www.beartreasures.com
Bear-a-thought	- www.bear-a-thought.co.uk
Bearable Bears	- www.bearablebears.nl
bearartistsofbritain.org	- www.bearartistsofbritain.org
Bearitz	- www.bearitz.com
Bearly Sane Bears	- www.bearlysanebears.com
Bearly There	- www.bearlythere.com
Bears 'n' Things	- www.bearsnthings.co.uk
Bears of Bath	- www.bearsofbath.co.uk
Bears of Eastwood	- http://web.mac.com/bearsofeastwood
Bears of the Abbey	- www.bearsoftheabbey.com
Bears of Windy Hill	- www.bearsofwindyhill.co.uk
Bears on the Square	- www.bearsonthesquare.com
Bears To Collect	- www.bears2collect.co.uk
Bears upon Soar	- www.bearsuponsoar.co.uk
Beary Cheap Bear Supplies	- www.bearycheap.com
Beary Special Supplies	- www.woodlandteddies.co.uk
Beatrix Bears	- www.beatrixbears.co.uk
BeauT Bears	- www.beautbears.nl
Beautifully Bear	- www.beautifully-bear.co.uk
Beavis, I C Ltd	- www.beavis-shops.co.uk
Bebbin Bears	- www.bebbinbears.co.uk
Beddingfield Bears	- www.beddingfieldbears.co.uk
Bedford Bears	- www.bedfordbears.co.uk
Bedspring Bears	- www.bedspringbears.com
Bedstead Bears	- www.bedsteadbears.com
Bee Antiques and Collectables	- www.bbears.co.uk
Bees Knees Bears	- www.beeskneesbears.co.uk
Benjamin Bears	- www.benjaminbears.bravehost.com
Berry Lane Bears	- www.berrylanebears.co.uk
BigFeetBears	- www.bigfeetbears.com
Billy Buff Bears	- www.billybuffbears.com
Bisson Bears	- www.bissonbears.com
Bobbys Bears	- www.bobbysbears.co.uk
Bonhams	- www.bonhams.com/toys
Bonsall Bears	- www.bonsallbears.com
Born Again Bears	- www.bornagainbears.co.uk
Bourton Bears	- www.bourtonbears.com
Box Bears	- www.boxbears.co.uk

Bradgate Bears	-	www.bradgatebears.co.uk
Bradley Bears	-	www.bradleybears.co.uk
Braveheart Bears	-	www.braveheartbears.co.uk
Brewer's Bruins	-	www.BrewersBruins.com
Brierley Bears	-	www.freewebs.com/brierleybears
British Bear Collection, The	-	www.thebritishbearcollection.co.uk
British Bear Fair	-	www.wendysworldfairs.co.uk
British Toymakers Guild	-	www.toymakersguild.co.uk
Brotherwood Bears	-	www.brotherwoodbears.com
Broughty Bears	-	www.broughtybears.co.uk
Browne Bears & Friends	-	www.brownebears.org.uk
Bruins All Roond	-	www.whiskers.eclipse.co.uk
Buckie Bears	-	www.buckiebears.co.uk
Bucks Bears	-	www.bucks-bears.co.uk
Bumble Bears	-	www.bumblebears.co.uk
Bunky Bears	-	www.BunkyBears.co.uk
burlingtonbears.com	-	www.burlingtonbears.com
Burra Bears	-	www.burrabears.co.uk
Button Bears	-	www.buttonbears.nl
Cala Bear Den	-	www.calabear.ca
Calico Pie	-	www.calicopie.co.uk
Calico Teddy, The	-	www.calicoteddy.com
Candi Bears	-	www.candibears.co.uk
Canterbury Bears	-	www.canterburybears.com
Caramac Bears	-	www.freewebs.com/caramacbears
Carmichael Bears	-	www.carmichaelbears.co.uk
Carol's Tiny Treasures	-	www.carolstinytreasures.co.uk
Causeway House Crafts	-	www.cinnamon-bear.co.uk
CC Bears Australia	-	www.ccbearsaustralia.com
Ce Gifts & Bears	-	www.cegifts.co.uk
Cejais Bears & Dollshouses	-	www.cejais.net
Charlie Bears Limited	-	www.charliebears.com
Chatham Village Bears L.L.C.	-	www.chathamvillagebears.com
Cheltenham Bears	-	www.cheltenhambears.co.uk
Childhood Fantasies	-	www.childhoodfantasiesbear.com
Christie Bears Limited	-	www.christiebears.co.uk
Christine Pike Bears	-	www.christinepike.com
Christmas Angels	-	www.christmasangels.co.uk
Clemens Bears of Germany	-	www.clemens-spieltiere.de
Cobblestone Bears and Gifts	-	www.blakemere-shoppingexperience.com
Colyns Cottage Bears	-	www.colynscottagebears.co.uk
Conradi Creations	-	www.conradicreations.com
Cornelia Bears - Holland	-	www.corneliabears.com
Country Bears	-	www.freewebs.com/country-bears
Cowslip Bear Company	-	www.cowslipbears.co.uk
Creations Past	-	www.dollshousewallpaper.co.uk
Cripple Creek Creative	-	www.cripplecreekcreative.com

Gorge Bear Company	-	www.bear-world.com
Grace Daisy Bears	-	www.lorrainemorris.com
Granny's Goodies	-	www.grannysgoodiesfairs.com
Great Bear 2008. The	-	www.jouetmusee.com
Greenleaf Bears	-	www.greenleafbears.co.uk
Gregory Bear	-	www.hugoshouse.com
Growlers Teddy Bears	-	www.growlers-teddybears.co.uk
Guardian Angel Bears	-	www.guardianangelbears.com
Gund (UK) Limited	-	www.gund.com
Hairy Hugs	-	www.hairyhugs.co.uk
Halcyon of St. Marychurch	-	www.halcyonbears.com
Hamleys of London	-	www.hamleys.com
Hand Glass Craft	-	www.handglasscraft.com
Hannay Bears, FJ.	-	www.fjhannaybears.com
Hansa Toys	-	www.hansa-uk.com
Happy Tymes® Collectibles	-	www.happytymes.net
Happy Tymes® Collectibles	-	www.www.teddiestogo.net
Hartley's of Leyburn	-	www.hartleybears.co.uk
Haven Bears	-	www.havenbears.com
Helmbold, A GmbH	-	www.A-Helmbold.de
Hen Nest, The	-	www.hennest.com
Hermann Teddy Original	-	www.teddy-hermann.de
Hildegard Gunzel Bears	-	www.hildegardguenzel.com
Holdingham Bears	-	www.holdinghambears.com
Hugglets	-	www.hugglets.co.uk
Hugs Unlimited	-	www.hugsunlimited.co.uk
Humble-Crumble Collectors Bears	-	www.victoriaallum.co.uk
Huntersfield Bears	-	www.huntersfieldbears.com
Inge Bears	-	www.ingebears.homestead.com
Inspirations	-	www.inspirationsgiftshop.co.uk
Isabelle Bears	-	www.enchantedwood.net
Izzy's Cubs	-	www.izzyscubs.com
J. C. W. Bears & Furry Friends	-	www.jcwbears.co.uk
Jac-q-Lyn Bears	-	www.jacqlynbears.com
Jeannette - Teddies Galore	-	www.jeannetteteddiesgalore.co.uk
JennyLovesBenny Bears	-	www.jennylovesbenny.com
Jo-Anne Bears	-	www.jo-annebears.co.uk
Joxy Bears	-	www.joxybears.co.uk
Joybunnys Art Designs	-	www.joybunnysartdesigns.co.uk
K M Bears	-	www.kmbears.co.uk
Karin Kronsteiner Bears	-	www.karinkronsteiner.at.tt
Kaz Bears	-	www.kazbears.com
KerrowBears	-	www.kerrowbears.co.uk
Kesseys Bears	-	www.kesseysbears.com
Keuns & Bears	-	http://users.skynet.be/keunsandbears
Kevinton Bears	-	www.kevintonbears.com
Kidman, Martin	-	www.martinkidman.com

Kingston Bears	-	www.kingstonbears.com
Kingswear Bears and Friends	-	www.kingswearbears.com
Knutty Bears	-	www.knuttybears.com
Koko's Bear Shop	-	www.kokosbearshop.com
L J Bears	-	www.ljbears.co.uk
L'Ours du Marais	-	www.oursdumarais.com
Latimer of Bewdley	-	www.latimerofbewdley.com
Laurie Lou Bears	-	www.laurieloubears.com
Leggat, Elizabeth	-	www.elizabethleggat.co.uk
Leigh Toy Fair	-	www.leightoyfair.co.uk
Life Like Friends	-	www.lifelikefriends.co.uk
Lillian Trigg of Rochester	-	www.lilliantrigg.co.uk
Lin à l'Ours, De	-	www.lin-ours.com
Little Acorns	-	www.littleacorns.org.uk
Little Paws	-	www.littlepawsludlow.co.uk
Little Scruffs of Evesham	-	www.miniaturemohairbears.co.uk
LoraBears	-	www.lorabears.com
Lucky Bears Limited	-	www.luckybears.com
Lyndee-Lou-Bears	-	www.lyndee-lou-bears.com
Lyrical Bears	-	www.lyrical-bears.co.uk
Mac Bears	-	www.macbears.co.uk
Madabout Bears	-	www.aldesign.freeserve.co.uk
Madeleine's Mini Bears	-	www.madeleineminibears.com
Majacabus Bears	-	www.majacabusbears.co.uk
Malu-Bear	-	www.malu-baer.de
Mary Myrtle Minatures	-	www.marymyrtleminiatures.co.uk
Mary Shortle	-	www.maryshortleofyork.com
Mawspaws	-	www.mawspaws.com
Maypole Bears by Jean	-	www.maypolebears.co.uk
Meadows Teddy Bears	-	www.ebay.co.uk/bearingifts07
Megelles	-	www.megelles.com
Melissa Jayne Bears	-	www.melissajaynebears.co.uk
Memory Lane	-	www.memorylanebears.co.uk
Merrythought Ltd	-	www.merrythought.co.uk
Midnight Bears	-	www.midnight-bears.co.uk
Milford Models & Hobbies	-	www.milford-models.co.uk
Minikins	-	www.maggiesminikins.com
Mirkwood Bears	-	www.mirkwoodbears.co.uk
Miss B's Bears	-	www.missbeesbears.com
Mister Bear	-	www.misterbear.net
Nadja Bears	-	www.nadjabears.be
Netty's Bears	-	www.jannettysbears.co.uk
Nobodys Bear	-	www.nobodysbear.eu
Okidoki Original	-	www.okidokioriginal.com
Old Bear Company	-	www.oldbearcompany.com
Old Bears Network	-	www.oldbearsnetwork.co.uk
Old Palace Antiques	-	www.old-palace-antiques.com

Old Time Bears	-	www.oldtimebears.com
Oldbearscene.com	-	www.oldbearscene.com
Olde Teddy Bear Shoppe, The	-	www.theoldeteddybearshoppe.com
Oops! Pardon me, Bears!	-	http://eileenwood.bta.com/oops
Orchard Bears	-	www.orchardbears.com
Original Rica-Bear	-	www.rica-bear.de
Orphan Bears	-	www.orphanbears.com
Oyster Box, The	-	www.theoysterbox.co.uk
Party Bears	-	www.partybears-bath.co.uk
Paw Prints of Staffordshire	-	www.pawprints.org.uk
PCBangles	-	www.pcbangles.co.uk
Peacock Fibres Ltd	-	www.noblecraft.co.uk
Pearson, Sue	-	www.suepearson.co.uk
Pearson, Sue	-	www.sue-pearson.co.uk
Pebble Beach Bears	-	www.pebblebeachbears.co.uk
Peek-A-Boo Teddy Bears	-	www.peekabooteddybears.co.uk
Peers, Louise	-	www.louisepeers.blogspot.com
Peggotty	-	www.peggotty.f9.co.uk
Penny Bunn Bears	-	www.pennybunnbears.co.uk
Perm Teddy Bear Club	-	www.teddyclub.narod.ru
Pertinax Bears	-	www.pertinaxbears.co.uk
Pick-me Bears	-	www.pick-me-bears.com
Piece Parade	-	www.pieceparade.com
Pied Piper, The	-	www.bearsanddolls.co.uk
Pijangi Bears	-	www.pijangibears.dk
Pipaluck Bears	-	www.pipaluck.co.uk
Pipedream Bears	-	www.bearsandpugs.com
Pipkins Bears	-	www.pipkinsbears.com
Pixel's Bears	-	www.pixelsbears.com
Pongo's Bears	-	www.pongosbears.co.uk
Postal Bears	-	www.postalbears.co.uk
Probär GmbH	-	www.probear.com
Pumpkin & Pickle Bears	-	www.pumpkinandpickle.co.uk
Puppenhausmuseum	-	www.puppenhausmuseum.ch
Puzzle Bears	-	www.puzzlebears.com
Quinn, Sue	-	www.bearsbysuequinn.co.uk
QVC	-	www.qvcuk.com
Rabbit Maker, The	-	www.therabbitmaker.com
Rainey Days	-	www.rainey-days.com
Rauch, Annette	-	www.annette-rauch.com
Razzle Dazzle	-	www.razzledazzlegifts.co.uk
Recollect Dolls Hospital	-	www.dollshospital.co.uk
Red or Ted	-	www.redorted.co.uk
Remem-bear Artist Bears	-	www.remembear.com
Restoration and Teddy Bear Artist	-	www.teddy-bear-artists.com/LB-home.htm
Robin Rive Bears	-	www.robinrive.com
Rosie's Attic	-	www.rosiesattic.co.uk

END

Bear Business Phone Directory

A

A Better Class of Bear 01189 713182
Abbey Bears. 01841 532484
Abbey Bears. 01503 265441
Abelia Bears. 01992 478229
Abracadabra Teddy Bears . . 01799 527222
Actually Bears by Jackie . . . 01449 675951
Admiral Bears Supplies 01372 813558
Alexander Bears. 01322 337797
All Bear by Paula Carter . . . 01622 686970
All Things Beary 0131 477 6970
All You Can Bear. 020 8368 5491
Allsorts of Bears 01263 514111
Always Bearing in Mind 01494 437238
AM Bears 07837 194433
Amanda's Honey Pot Bears 028 207 42927
AngieBears. 01634 253165
Ann Made Bears 020 8202 3165
Ann_Knits 4 Bears 02380 846987
Ann's Ridgehill Bears. 01233 721900
Anna Koetse's Bears . . +31 (0)23 5472048
Apple Pie House Ltd 01531 635290
Arctophilia 01795 597770
Around The Garden Bears. . 01273 585259
Arundel Teddy Bears. 0776 997 7195
Ashby Bears & Collectables. 01530 564444
Ashwood Nurseries 01384 401996
Asquiths 01753 831200
Atlantic Bears. 01445 712179
Aurorabearealis 01463 731470

B

B-Bears And Gifts . . . . +61 (0)7 3325 5366
Ba's Bears 01865 435314
Bacton Bears 01449 781087
Baggaley Bears. 0115 8757 031
Bailey Bears. 01923 673437
Balu Bears. . . . . +49 (0) 531 34 26 90
Bar Street Bears 01723 353636
Barbara-Ann Bears 01303 269038
Bärenboutique . . . . +49 (0)1577 316 26 46
Bärenhäusl-Ositos-Bären . . . .
. . . . +49 (0)80 61 34 33 10
Barling Bears 01732 845059

Barnwell Bears. 01244 380422
Barrel Bears 01384 410438
Barron Bears . . . . +1 760 598 9123
Baybee Bears. 07729 117410
Bear Bahoochie 01324 411823
Bear Basics 01963 364777
Bear Bits. 01507 578360
Bear Crazee 0798 607 2712
The Bear Emporium 01142 482010
The Bear Garden 01483 302581
The Bear Huggery 01624 676333
Bear in Mind. 01304 366234
Bear It In Mind 01590 612097
The Bear Patch 01335 342391
Bear Paths. . . . . +1 216 566 1519
Bear Pawtraits 0780 3780050
The Bear Shop. 01206 577345
The Bear Shop. 01603 766866
The Bear Supplies Company . . . .
. . . . 0191 584 1111
Bear Treasures. 01942 862354
Bear-a-thought 01207 563220
Bearable Bears. . . . . . +31 (0)55 5788067
bearartistsofbritain.org 07725 640179
Bearitz 01828 670561
Bearly Sane Bears 01752 403515
Bearly There. 01384 236532
Bearnoni Bears . . . . . . +27 (0)11 849 1825
Bears 'n' Things 01942 234222
Bears & Stitches 01394 388999
Bears Abundant . . . . +1 416 493 2944
Bears by Eunice 020 8205 6308
Bears by Hand 01536 461159
Bears by Julia 01206 386654
Bears by Julie-Ann 0121 602 0443
Bears by Susan Jane Knock. 01376 521230
The Bears Den. 01709 828619
Bears N' Company. . . . . . +1 705 726 1499
Bears of Bath 01761 417271
Bears of Eastwood. 01482 847535
Bears of the Abbey . . . . . +1 416 703 1697
Bears of Windy Hill. 01274 599175
Bears on the Square 01952 433924
Bears Paw Collectables . . . 0116 274 1441

Bears To Collect. 01480 860376
Bears Unlimited 01590 670536
Bears upon Soar 01509 670481
Bears With Attitude 01332 690624
Beary Cheap Bear Supplies . . . .
. . . . +61 (0)7 5520 3455
Beary Special Supplies 01509 267597
Beatrix Bears 01743 340276
BeauT Bears . . . . +31 (0)610 623 559
Beautifully Bear 07765 381951
C J Beavis Ltd 01234 353741
I C Beavis Ltd. 01983 523271
Bebbin Bears 01296 423755
Bebes et Jouets 01289 304802
Beddingfield Bears. 0796 3723220
Bedford Bears 01767 318626
Bedraggle Bears™ 0117 9497389
Bedspring Bears . . . . . . +34 922 701 004
Bee Antiques and Collectables . . . .
. . . . 01843 864040
Bees Knees Bears 01902 843124
Bell Bears 020 8778 0217
Belly Button Bears 01487 842538
Benjamin Bears 01634 832523
Berry Lane Bears. 01268 558007
Bessy Bears. 07900 815445
Beth's Bears. 01355 249674
Betty's Bears 01267 221721
Big Tree Bears 0115 952 4022
BigFeetBears 07855 209293
Bilbo Bears 0161 794 7931
Billy Buff Bears . . . . +34 972 770923
Bisson Bears . . . . +47 47967755
Bobbys Bears. 01204 468090
Bobbys Bears Fairs 01204 697419
Bolebridge Bears 01827 59097
Bonhams 08700 273627
Bonsall Bears 0114 2508532
Born Again Bears 01329 313786
Bourton Bears 01452 760186
Box Bears. 07956 555230
Bracken Bears 01929 554055
Bradgate Bears 0116 236 7147
Bradley Bears. 01406 373073
Brewer's Bruins . . . . +1 704 433 6507
Bridgwater Bears 01473 412066
Brierley Bears. 07841 159666
The British Bear Collection . 01934 822263
British Bear Fair 01895 834348
British Toymakers Guild 01225 442440

Brooklyn Bears. 01604 891585
Brotherwood Bears 01249 760284
Broughty Bears 01382 477567
Brow Bears. 01229 467861
Browne Bears & Friends . . . 016973 20484
Buckie Bears 01542 835639
Bucks Bears. 01628 472735
Bumble Bears. 02380 326663
Bunky Bears. 01636 678724
Burlington Bearties. 01384 279731
burlingtonbears.com. 0870 0671873
Burra Bears 01595 859374
Button Bears. . . . . +31 (0)612 439297

C

Cala Bear Den . . . . +1 204 257 6003
Calico Pie. 01524 412460
The Calico Teddy. . . . . . +1 410 433 9202
Candi Bears 01563 830729
Canterbury Bears. 01227 728630
Caramac Bears 01780 767183
Carmichael Bears. 01928 563874
Carol's Tiny Treasures 01454 318573
Causeway House Crafts . . . 01433 620343
CC Bears Australia . . . . . +61 3 5759 2574
Ce Gifts & Bears 01629 814811
Cejais Bears & Dollshouses. 024 76 633630
Chapple Bears 01736 755577
Charlie Bears Limited. 01409 271420
Chatham Village Bears L.L.C. . . . .
. . . . +1 314 739 8426
Cheltenham Bears 07905 307859
Cherry's Chums . . . . +34 928163269
Chesney Designs 01524 733152
Chester Bears 01978 855604
Childhood Fantasies . . . . +1 304 260 0658
Christie Bears Limited 01656 789054
Christine Pike Bears 01366 380229
Christmas Angels 01904 639908
Clemens Bears of Germany. 01246 269723
Cleopatra Bears 01738 638933
Cobblestone Bears and Gifts. 01606 889192
Colyns Cottage Bears 01592 566621
Conradi Creations 020 8671 2794
Cornelia Bears - Holland. . . . .
. . . . +31 (0)70 32 95 857
Cornwall and Devon Bear Fairs . . . .
. . . . 01208 872251
Country Bears 01934 811785
Courses with Bear Bits. 01507 578360

Coventry Bears 07947 066675
Cowslip Bear Company 01202 382073
Creations Past 01905 820792
Crotchety Bears 01562 752289
Cuddly Kerrlectables 01349 854256
Cuddy Lugs 01386 858134
Curtis Brae of Stratford 01789 267277
Cynnaman Restoration Services. . . . .
. . . . 01268 754184

D

Daisa Original Designs Ltd . 01652 661881
Daphne Fraser's...Bear Hospital. . . . .
. . . . 0141 776 1281
Dari Laut Bears 01424 754418
Dashing Duck . . . . . . +33 (0)4 68 49 15 67
Dean's Collectors Club. 01981 240966
Dean's Rag Book Co (1903) Ltd. . . . .
. . . . 01981 240966
Di Nic's Bears . . . . +61 (0)2 665 12463
Anna Dickerson 01603 759647
Do Do Bears 01206 524261
Doll & Teddy Fairs 01530 274377
Dolls Designs 01903 602988
Dolls, Bears and Bygones . . 07889 630051
Dolly Daydreams 01256 889111
Dolly Domain of South Shields . . . .
. . . . 0191 42 40 400
Dolly Land. 020 8360 1053
Dolly Mixtures 0121 422 6959
Dolly's Daydreams 01945 870160
Doodlebears & Friends 01296 397082
The Dorset Teddy Bear Museum . . . .
. . . . 01305 266040
Dot Bird 01765 607131
Drawing the Web 01303 269038
Dream House . . . . . . +33 (0)4 93 55 09 16
Dreamtime . . . . 020 8842 2327 (Bear)
Drury Bears 01732 364042
Véronique Dubosc. . . +33 (0)5 56 51 04 65
durrerBears and more . +61 (0)8 9368 1557
Dusty Attic Bears 01458 860532

E

E. J. Bears 01992 714354
EcoBears. . . . . +34 617 836 923
Eden Bears 01524 418377
Eildon Bears. 01896 823832
Elizbet Bears 01633 615208
Ellie-Bears 01268 762438

Emmary Bears 01208 872251
Enchanted Place Bears 01326 210462
Eskole Noombas. . . . . +65 6545 5904
Essential Bears . . . . . . +27 (0)21 685 3487
Evolution Bears. 0151 678 9452

F

Fair Bears. 01909 564472
Fairyland Bears 07720 957072
Farnborough Bears 01252 543454
FenBeary Folk. 0845 157 6871
Fine and Dandy Bears 01476 550079
Flutter-By Bears 01782 560136
Forest Glen Bears 07967 972611
Fred-I-Bear. . . . . +27 (0)83 2500378Fredi's
Workbasket. . . . . +27 (0)83 2500378
Futch Bears 01277 219032

G

G & T Evans Woodwool 01686 622100
G-Rumpy Bears 020 8275 0693
Garrington Bears 01622 685194
Gemstone Bears 01637 877743
Geraldine's of Edinburgh . . 0131 333 1833
The Gift 01636 610075
Gill's Gollies 01733 702490
The Glass Eye Co. 01492 642220
Glendaveny Teddy Bears. . . 01779 481608
Goldilocks. 01425 403558
Golly Galore 01227 760186
Good Bears of the World . . . 01934 822342
Gorge Bear Company 01934 743333
Grace Daisy Bears. 01256 476140
Granny Grumps Bears 01502 715347
Granny's Goodies 020 8693 5432
The Great Bear 2008 +33 (0)4 66 57 25 13
Greenleaf Bears. 01543 877343
Jo Greeno 01483 224312
Gregory Bear 01932 243263
Greta May Antiques 01732 366730
Growlers Teddy Bears 01392 276891
Guardian Angel Bears 01637 881114
Gund (UK) Limited 01772 629292
Gyll's Bears. 0208 366 1836

H

H M Bears 01524 733152
Hairy Hugs 07765 434441
Halcyon of St. Marychurch. . 01803 314958

Hamleys of London 020 7479 7308
Hampton Bears 01453 872615
Hand Glass Craft 01384 573410
F.J. Hannay Bears 01642 480622
Hansa Toys 020 8954 5956
Happy Tymes® Collectibles . . . .
. . . . +1 610 873 0407
Hardy Bears 01590 670615
Hartley's of Leyburn 01969 622209
Leanda Harwood 01529 300737
Haven Bears 01928 788313
Hazelwood Bears 01342 712413
Heavenly Creations 01425 470654
A Helmbold GmbH . . . +49 (0)36946 22009
The Hen Nest . . . . +1 334 696 3480
Hermann Teddy Original +49 (0)9543 84820
Hermann Teddy Original . . . 0208 954 5956
Hildegard Gunzel Bears 01246 269723
Hilltop Toys 01722 712265
Hoblins 01772 635516
Holdingham Bears 01529 303266
Holly Bears 01889 568848
Honey Pot Bears 02392 472455
Hovvigs . . . . +45 5991 3494
Hug-A-Boo Bears 01460 72740
Hugglets 01273 697974
Huggy Bears 07796 952427
Hugs Unlimited 01706 839938
Humble-Crumble 01702 715383
Huntersfield Bears 01209 711557
Hyefolk 01303 277925

I

Inge Bears . . . . +27 (0)721 104273
Inspirations 01252 336677
Izzy's Cubs 01756 796548

J

J.C.W. Bears & Furry Friends 01268 726558
Jac-Q-Lyn Bears 01260 224257
Jac-Q-Lyn Bears 01538 388831
Jan's Tiddy Bears 07889 794637
Jasco Bears 01704 539324
Jeannette - Teddies Galore . 0208 958 6101
Jenni Bears 01625 877184
JennyLovesBenny Bears . . . .
. . . . +61 (0)422 852 236
Jo-Anne Bears 01621 815049
Jodie's Bears . . . . +81 (0)466 25 1202
Joxy Bears 01964 533096

Joybunnys Art Designs 07971 076259
Ju-Beary Bears 01268 525775
Just Golly Collectors Club . . 01903 721070

K

K M Bears 0113 2192651
Karin Kronsteiner Bears . . . .
. . . . +43 (0)316 83 91 82
Kaysbears by Kay Street . . . 01474 351757
Kaytkins 01933 355782
Kaz Bears 01332 731948
KerrowBears 07971 525377
Kesseys Bears 01745 356254
Keuns & Bears . . . . +32 (0)59 800777
Kevinton Bears 07957 333044
Martin Kidman 01273 842938
Kieron James Designs 01444 484870
Kingston Bears 01425 470654
Kingswear Bears and Friends 01803 752632
Knutty Bears 01626 863032
Koko's Bear Shop 01983 616815

L

L J Bears 01590 676517
L'Ours du Marais . . . . +33 (0)1 42 77 60 43
Latimer of Bewdley 01299 404000
Laurie Lou Bears 01603 890819
Leeds Doll & Teddy Fair . . . 0191 42 40 400
Elizabeth Leggat 01355 249674
Leigh Toy Fair 01702 473288
Reinhold Lesch GmbH 020 7794 2377
Let's Go Round Again 01902 324141
Life Like Friends 0118 956 8877
Lillian Trigg of Rochester . . . 01634 713131
De Lin à l'Ours . . . . . +33 (0)3 80 35 46 77
Little Acorns 01633 271010
Little Paws 01584 875286
Little Scruffs of Evesham . . . 01386 429002
LoraBears . . . . +1 323 445 3428
Loteni Bears 01493 731401
Love is in the Bear 020 8304 1412
Lucky Bears Limited 01702 204182
Lynda Brown Bears 020 8570 0095
Lyndee-Lou-Bears 01624 616475
Lyrical Bears 01438 351651

M

Mac Bears by Carol Davidson . . . .
. . . . 020 8863 6192
Madabout Bears 01294 835432

Madeleine's Mini Bears . . . .
. . . . +33 (0)1 39 14 50 86
Majacabus Bears 01458 832008
Malu-Bear . . . . +49 (0)7151 72769
Marigold Bears 01564 776092
Mary Shortle 01904 425168
Mawspaws 01296 338338
Maypole Bears 01386 48217
Meadows Teddy Bears 01204 693087
Megelles . . . . +61 7 3720 0850
Meldrum Bears 01726 74499
Melissa Jayne Bears 01606 782183
Memory Lane 01422 833223
Merrythought Ltd 01952 433116
Midnight Bears 07864 120945
Milford Models & Hobbies . . 01590 642112
Minikins by Maggie Spackman . . . .
. . . . +1 843 875 2565
Mirkwood Bears 01225 356505
Miss B's Bears 01829 271873
Mister Bear 01702 710733
Muffti Hugs 01908 643679

N

Nadja Bears . . . . +32 (0)3 568 15 15
Namtloc Bears 01429 422997
Narnie Bears 07903 082630
Netty's Bears 01372 813558
New Forest Bears 01726 76505
noBodys Bear 01726 824136
Normandy Bears . . . . +33 (0)2 33 55 98 61

O

Okidoki Original . . . . +46 (0)46 142089
The Old Bear Company Ltd . 01246 862387
Old Bears Network 01422 823079
Old Palace Antiques 01208 872909
Old Time Bears 01843 593619
Oldbearscene 01892 521232
The Olde Teddy Bear Shoppe . . . .
. . . . +1 905 893 3590
Oops! Pardon me, Bears! . . 01476 563599
Orchard Bears 01494 717501
Original Rica-Bear® . . . +49 (0)5231 59750
Orphan Bears 01707 649758
Out of the Woods© 01737 821218
The Oyster Box 01622 685423

P

Pam Howells 01778 344152

Panda Jak Bears . . . . +353 (0)94 938 0962
Parade - The Gift Shop 01223 578728
Party Bears 01225 446097
Paw Prints of Staffordshire . 01782 537315
Paws in the Forest 02380 282697
PCBangles 07931 216695
Peacock Fibres Ltd 01274 633900
Sue Pearson 01273 774851
Pebble Beach Bears 01273 277747
Peek-A-Boo Teddy Bears . . 020 8855 4499
Louise Peers 01625 527917
Peggotty . . . . +1 972 491 0104
Pennbeary 01367 252809
Penny Bunn Bears 01453 828060
Nicola Perkins 01782 751077
Petal Originals 01372 724386
Pick-me Bears . . . . +49 (0)89 6924102
The Piece Parade . . . . . . +1 919 870 1881
The Pied Piper 01242 251532
Pijangi Bears . . . . +45 5626 8320
Pipaluck Bears 07966 162650
Pipedream Bears 0161 285 8254
Pippawicks 01424 428676
Pixel's Bears 01584 890472
Pogmear Bears 07730 788581
Pongo's Bears 07952 578224
Postal Bears 01457 766650
The Potting Shed 01534 854203
Probär GmbH . . . . +49 (0)2562 7013 0
Pumpkin & Pickle Bears . . . 01892 652706
Puppenhausmuseum . +41 (0)61 225 95 95
Puzzle Bears 01483 224524
Pywacket Teddies 023 9245 2266

Q

Sue Quinn 0141 887 9916
QVC 0800 514131

R

The Rabbit Maker 01772 811254
Rainey Days Old Bears & Friends . . . .
. . . . 020 8647 6235
Ramshackle Bears 01273 454746
Annette Rauch . . . . . . +49 (0)36781 40363
Razzle Dazzle 01179 614141
Ready Tedi Go! 01444 413487
Recollect Dolls Hospital 01444 871052
Red or Ted 07875 498763
Remem-bear Artist Bears . . . 07624 489906
Restoration and Teddy Bear Artist . . . .

. . . . +1 414 871 4956
Rhiw Valley Bears 01686 650883
Robin Rive Bears 0121 288 0548
The Rocking Horse Gallery +1 540 371 1894
Rosie's Attic 07776 191960
Round About Bears 01502 578338
Rowan Bears 01903 240467
Ruben Bears 01582 731544
Running Bear Company . . . .
. . . . +49 (0)491 912 1526
Pat Rush 01732 361994

S

Sad Pad Bears. 01622 754441
Sally Anne Bears 01522 509329
Sally B Gollies 0118 9775464
Sambrook Bears 01268 562163
Sarah Bears. . . . . +1 719 839 5770
Sarah's Bears of Cambridge 01223 566960
Sarah's Bruins 01945 461257
Scruffie Bears by Susan Pryce . . . .
. . . . 01244 534724
Scruffy Bears 01903 734865
Scrumpy Bears. 01460 52002
Seashore Bears 01292 288252
Send 2 Mend Bears 01945 475201
Serendipity 01422 340097
Sew What & Stuff It 01925 725084
Shantock Bears 01442 260486
Shebob Bears 01342 714568
Julie Shepherd 01730 810878
Shultz Characters. 01329 834681
Sixpenny Bears 01539 436003
Snazzy Gollys 01903 721070
Southway Bears 01425 654768
Springer Bears 01773 748093
St Ann's Dolls Hospital 01494 890220
St Martin's Gallery 01425 489090
Stanley Bears . . . . +61 (0)3 5728 6623
Starlite Bears 07802 568685
Margarete Steiff GmbH . +49 (0)7322 131-1
Steiff Gallery 0208 466 8444
Steiff UK. 01483 266643
Studio 44 . . . . 01775 820429

T

Tamerton Teddys 01752 480656
Teachers Pets 01284 704253
Teddies 2008 . . . . 01273 697974
Teddies and Chums 01525 635372

Teddies of Trenode 01503 240462
The Teddy Bear Chest 07913 872721
Teddy Bear Club International . . . .
. . . . 01903 884988
The Teddy Bear Club Store . 08700 347578
Teddy Bear Hollow 0845 388 3021
Teddy Bear House 01305 263200
The Teddy Bear Orphanage. 01744 812274
Teddy Bear Review . . . . . +1 715 445 5000
Teddy Bear Scene Magazine. 01778 391158
Teddy Bears & Friends of Bourne. . . . .
. . . . 01778 426898
Teddy Bears Downstairs +61 (0)2 4933 9794
Teddy Bears Home 01442 267328
Teddy Bears of Witney 01993 706616
Teddy Bears UK. 01992 309282
Teddy Bears' Picknick. . +31 (0)343 577068
Teddy Bearsville 0121 559 9990
Teddy Lane. 01636 816017
Teddy's Room . . . . +49 162 4321132
Teddytech . . . . +27 (0)31 312 7755
Tedi Enfys. 01633 780247
Tedi Ty Coed 01443 776031
Teds of the Riverbank 0161 303 0011
Teeny Bears 02380 446356
Terry's Teddy Hospital 01438 718700
Tewin's Bruins 01438 718700
The Bear Necessities - Knarf-Bears . . . . . .
. . . . +32 (0)5034 1027
The Teddy Shop 01992 309282
Prue Theobalds 01424 422306
The Thing About Bears 01304 369253
Elizabeth Thompson. 01993 811915
Thoughts 01782 641919
Threadteds . . . . +31 (0)77 3984960
Three O'Clock Bears. 024 7641 6654
Tillington Bears. 01223 837701
Tilly Bears. 07958 477326
Tiny Huggables Ltd 0207 3517139
Tiny Teddies by Ann 029 2075 3133
TinyBear . . . . +45 4444 1898
Toggle Teddies 01773 824258
TonniBears . . . . +31 592 262854
Top 'n' Tail Teddy Bears . . . 01304 363040
Torquay Teddies 07867 863664
Totally Teddies 01277 821890
Toto's. 0161 928 7657
The Toy Auctioneer 020 7870 8124
The Toy Chest 01768 891237
Toy Emporium 01746 765134

Toy Gallery 01482 864890
Toys of Youth 01234 841649
Toys...by Susan . . . . +1 416 242 6446
Traditional Toys Ltd 01443 222693
Trafford Print & Design. 01933 229366
Treasured Teddies 01295 690479
Trendle International Ltd . . . 01984 656825
Trevor Jenner Designer Jewellery . . . .
. . . . 01342 713858
Twilight Teds. 01925 725084

U

Urchins The Bear Shop 01840 250800

V

Valewood Bears 01274 883783
Vectis Auctions 01642 750616
Vera Bears . . . . +27 (0)11 788 3107
Very I Bears 07789 865920
Village Bears . . . . +1 941 366 2667

W

Warren Bears 01689 871420
Wealden Manor Press. 0118 941 4000
Wellfield Bears 02920 453045

Wellfields 02920 453045
Wellwood Bears 029 2073 6610
Westie Bears 01403 241381
Westmead Teddies. 01983 840643
Whittle-Le-Woods Bears . . . 01204 706831
Winklemoor Bears 01495 244528
The Winter BearFest 01273 697974
Wishing Well Bears. 0114 248 2010
Wooden Hill Bears 01225 442615
Woodgate Bears 01273 891665
Woodland Teddies 01509 267597
Woodrow Bears 01291 421369
Woodville Bears 01283 221829
Wookey Bears 01749 672243
World of Bears 01823 332050
The World Society for the Protection of
Animals 0800 316 9772

Y

Yesterday's Children 01945 440466

END

International Telephone Information

Dialling the UK from overseas

UK phone numbers in the Guide have been listed with their area dialling code, beginning with a zero. If dialling the UK from overseas please

• begin with your international dialling code
• then dial the UK dialling code – 44
• omit the zero from the start of the area code

Eg 01273 654321 should be dialled as:
Your international dialling code 44 1273 654321

Don't forget to check the time difference of the country you're phoning — to avoid calling in the middle of the night!

Dialling out from the UK - add 00

International phone numbers have been listed beginning with their country dialling code.
From the UK add the international dialling code –00– to the number. Eg +49 (0)987 12345 should be dialled as 00 49 987 12345, omiting the zero in brackets which only applies if within that country.
Phone numbers in display advertisements have been included as supplied to us and so may need careful attention to ensure they are dialled correctly; check your phone book for details about phoning abroad under International Information.
Particularly note differences in ringing & engaged tones.

Europe	GMT + 1 hour	W. Australia	GMT + 7-8 hours	New Zealand	GMT +12 hours
USA & Canada	GMT – 6-8 hours	E. Australia	GMT + 10 hours	Japan	GMT + 9 hours

Display Advertiser Index

END

Visiting a Hugglets Festival

To help you feel at home and make the most of your visit to a Hugglets Festival here are some practical tips. You'll probably find them helpful even if it's not your first time.

Those who arrive before the opening time of 11am will find a queue winding its way down towards Kensington High Street. Some people arrive very early as they are keen to get the best choice of bears from one or other artist but otherwise the main advantage to arriving much before 11am is the free chocolates passed down the line!

Before joining the queue we recommend you obtain your entry ticket from the Hugglets reception desk at the entrance to the halls. If you already have a ticket you can join the queue directly.

Tickets cost £4 on the day – but this 21st anniversary issue of the Guide contains two complimentary tickets for both events in 2008.

The queue often gets very long but despite this we usually manage to get everyone in within ten minutes because tickets are already held. If someone in the queue doesn't already have their ticket they just step aside when they get to reception – we sell as fast as possible but a short delay for these ticket buyers is inevitable.

The venue is suitable for wheelchair access (please come directly to reception via the entry point higher up Hornton Street to avoid external stairs). An internal lift is available between the three floors as well as the internal stairs. There are toilet facilities on both the top floor and basement but disabled toilet facilities are limited to the basement.

Before handing in your ticket at the door please make sure you complete the prize draw details on the back to stand a chance of winning one of four £50 vouchers to spend at the event. Winners are announced and invited to collect the voucher from reception. If you need to leave early don't worry – if you win a prize we'll post the voucher to you to spend at the next Hugglets Festival.

If at any time you need to leave the venue and return please ask for a pass-out card at the door as you go out. You might need to step outside because phone reception is patchy or for a bit of fresh air (or to smoke) or if you prefer to eat out at lunchtime.

If you have coats and bags with you can deposit these at the free cloakroom in the basement (hall 3). You can also use this facility if your purchases mount up during the day – but don't forget to collect them!

From the point you enter the event everything is open to you – over 10,000 teddy bears and related collectables on sale in an enormous variety of styles, sizes, colours, ages and prices.

The event takes place on all three floors and in four different halls. The ground floor has halls 1 and 2 (the first one you come to is actually hall two). The top floor is called hall 4 and the basement hall 3.

The number of stands in each hall is as follows:
Hall 1 - 67 stands
Hall 2 - 33 stands
Hall 3 - 36 stands
Hall 4 - 39 stands

Many people find it helpful to review the list of exhibitors before the event. A floor-plan showing exhibitor positions will be available on the day from the reception area. You can collect one when you arrive and review it while waiting in the queue. You can also use the floorplan on page 190 of this Guide and obtain the exhibitor list and stand numbers from the Hugglets website. It's a good idea to identify any stands you particularly want to visit early in the day when more bears are still available.

For about two months prior to a

Festival we also add links on our website to take you to the websites of our exhibitors. This is great for previewing the sorts of bears offered by each exhibitor. The links remain available on the site for about a year after the event to help you track down an exhibitor if you later regret not buying one of their bears!

If you are especially intent on buying a particular bear or a bear from a particular artist it may be worth contacting the exhibitor in advance in case a bear can be reserved, or perhaps you can buy in advance and collect on the day.

There are so many great bears it will be hard to know where to begin. Most of the leading teddy bear artists in the UK will be there.

Hugglets Festivals also offer a rare opportunity to meet bear artists and other exhibitors from overseas - so you'll not want to miss these. There are usually around 40 exhibitors from overseas. They are located through all the halls but can be readily identified on the printed exhibitor list by a round dot. Countries often repre-sented include Australia, Austria, Belgium, Canada, Germany, Ireland, Japan, South Africa, The Netherlands & USA.

A quick word about photography - if you want to take photos we won't be sur-prised because the displays are wonderful and the artistry amazing – but please ask permission of the exhibitor first.

The event hosts a charity stand on the

ground floor run by Good Bears of the World – hall 2 stand 75C. GBW provide new teddy bears to comfort those in distress. When they receive donations of older bears they sell them to raise funds for their worthwhile cause. You can find some great bears to adopt here.

Just past the reception area you'll see a bear repairer. Another is located on stand 75B. You may be lucky to find a repair can be done on the day but often teddies need to become in-patients.

If you are thinking of selling an old bear there are one or two stands who can give valuations for selling at auction. There are also are many dealers in old bears who would be pleased to see your bear and perhaps make an offer.

Not all exhibitors can take cheque or card payments, especially those from overseas, so it's a good idea to have sufficient cash for your proposed purchases. If you need to top up, the nearest cash points are on Kensington High Street.

By now you might be getting hungry! On the top floor you'll find the snack bar and licensed bar. Because the event is busy there may be delays in being served at peak times. An alternative is to take a break outside at one the local eateries or find a seat in the balcony area overlooking hall 1 and break out the sandwiches! If you do go out for food please note that fast food cannot be brought back into the premises so you'll need to finish it outside.

If you are coming with a party it is a good idea to arrange a meeting time and place in case you split up. Sorry, we generally won't make public announcements to reunite you with your friends, but we make an exception if children are lost.

On the subject of things being lost, please keep hold of your bags. You'll need to put them down to cuddle an irresistible bear from time to time but remember to pick them up again. If you do lose something please report it to the Hugglets reception at the entrance. We'll take your contact details and reunite you with your property if it is handed in. If you find something, please bring it to reception or if it is next to a stand please bring it to the attention of the exhibitor.

The event finishes at 4.30pm so you'll want to regroup and make sure you've visited all the halls before then. At 4.15pm we make an announcement to recommend you make your final purchases before the journey home. If you have left items in the cloakroom please collect them. Anything still there at the end of the day will be transferred to the Hugglets reception desk.

If you are hoping to get a taxi we advise you to walk down to main road and hail one from there. Phoning for a cab is not always successful.

If you have parked in the car park, you'll need to pay at the machine or at the manned booth before rejoining your car.

Have a safe journey back and we hope your adopted bears settle well into their new home!

Glenn & Irene Jackman,
Hugglets

END

2008 PUBLISHING **Hugglets** **2008**

Your complimentary tickets are on pages 191-193

Please see overleaf for floorplans

For exhibitor lists
& visitor information please see
www.hugglets.co.uk

Venue – Kensington Town Hall
Hornton Street, London, W8.

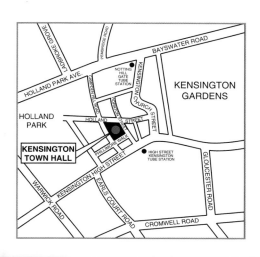

Entry times

11am - 4.30pm
Tickets at door:
£4 for adults,
£2 for children.

Parking is only £4
for the day.
400 spaces.
Nearest Tube is
High Street Kensington

Hugglets, PO Box 290, Brighton, BN2 1DR Tel: 01273 697974
Fax: 01273 62 62 55   Email: info@hugglets.co.uk www.hugglets.co.uk

Hugglets Festivals Floorplans

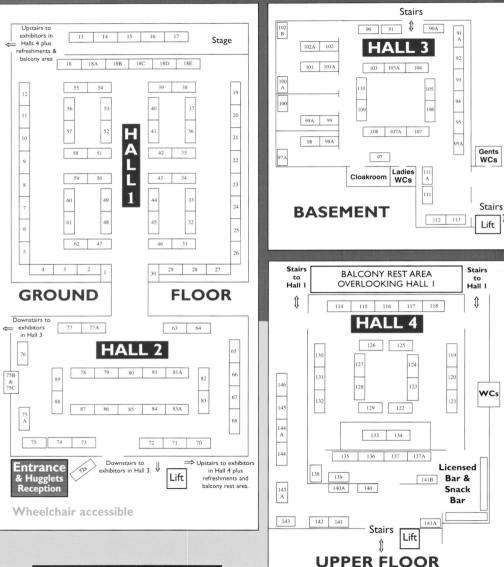

Upstairs to exhibitors in Halls 4 plus refreshments & balcony area

←

| 13 | 14 | 15 | 16 | 17 | Stage |

| 18 | 18A | 18B | 18C | 18D | 18E |

HALL 1

GROUND FLOOR

Downstairs to exhibitors in Hall 3 ←

HALL 2

Entrance & Hugglets Reception

Downstairs to exhibitors in Hall 3. ⇓ Lift

⇒ Upstairs to exhibitors in Hall 4 plus refreshments and balcony rest area.

Wheelchair accessible

Stairs ⇕

HALL 3

BASEMENT

Cloakroom | Ladies WCs | Gents WCs

Stairs ⇕ Lift

Stairs to Hall 1 ⇕ | BALCONY REST AREA OVERLOOKING HALL 1 | Stairs to Hall 1 ⇕

| 114 | 115 | 116 | 117 | 118 |

HALL 4

WCs

Licensed Bar & Snack Bar

Stairs ⇕ | Lift

UPPER FLOOR

FESTIVALS **Hugglets**

Please note Hugglets Festivals have been designated
NO SMOKING

For exhibitor lists: www.hugglets.co.uk

WINTER BEARFEST

Valid for adult or child entry from 11.00am – 4.30pm

24th February 2008

Kensington Town Hall, Hornton St., London W8
Extra tickets on sale at reception

Please enter the prize draw on the reverse of this ticket

Come to the Winter BearFest

... and bring a friend!

Please enter the prize draw on the reverse of this ticket

WINTER BEARFEST

Valid for adult or child entry from 11.00am – 4.30pm

24th February 2008

Kensington Town Hall, Hornton St., London W8
Extra tickets on sale at reception

Prize Draw - you could win £50!

Before handing in your ticket please complete details for your chance to win one of four £50 vouchers to spend at a Hugglets Festival. First draw at 12, then hourly. Your slip will be entered into all draws. Limited to one entry per person. Unclaimed winners will be notified by mail.

PLEASE ENTER CLEARLY:

Name ....

Address ....

Town ....

County ....

Postcode ....

Email (if any) ....

Prize Draw - you could win £50!

Before handing in your ticket please complete details for your chance to win one of four £50 vouchers to spend at a Hugglets Festival. First draw at 12, then hourly. Your slip will be entered into all draws. Limited to one entry per person. Unclaimed winners will be notified by mail.

PLEASE ENTER CLEARLY:

Name ....

Address ....

Town ....

County ....

Postcode ....

Email (if any) ....

TEDDIES
2008

MID SEPTEMBER

Valid for adult or child entry from 11.00am – 4.30pm

14th September 2008

Kensington Town Hall, Hornton St., London W8
Extra tickets on sale at reception

Please enter the prize draw on the reverse of this ticket

Come to Teddies 2008

... and bring a friend!

Please enter the prize draw on the reverse of this ticket

TEDDIES
2008

MID SEPTEMBER

Valid for adult or child entry from 11.00am – 4.30pm

14th September 2008

Kensington Town Hall, Hornton St., London W8
Extra tickets on sale at reception

Prize Draw - you could win £50!

Before handing in your ticket please complete details for your chance to win one of four £50 vouchers to spend at a Hugglets Festival. First draw at 12, then hourly. Your slip will be entered into all draws. Limited to one entry per person. Unclaimed winners will be notified by mail.

PLEASE ENTER CLEARLY:

Name ....

Address ....

Town ....

County ....

Postcode ....

Email (if any) ....

Prize Draw - you could win £50!

Before handing in your ticket please complete details for your chance to win one of four £50 vouchers to spend at a Hugglets Festival. First draw at 12, then hourly. Your slip will be entered into all draws. Limited to one entry per person. Unclaimed winners will be notified by mail.

PLEASE ENTER CLEARLY:

Name ....

Address ....

Town ....

County ....

Postcode ....

Email (if any) ....